ALEXANDER THE GREAT

The truth about Alexander the Great's life and political principles revealed

TABLE OF CONTENTS

The information herein is offered for informational purposes solely, and is universal as so. The presentation of the information is without contract or any type of guarantee assurance.

The trademarks that are used are without any consent, and the publication of the trademark is without permission or backing by the trademark owner. All trademarks and brands within this book are for clarifying purposes only and are the owned by the owners themselves, not affiliated with this document.

INTRODUCTION

The Greek city-states, the Greek kingdom of Macedon rose to power under Philip II. Alexander III, commonly known as Alexander the Great, was born to Philip II in Pella in 356 BCE and succeeded his father to the throne at the age of 20. He spent most of his ruling years on an unprecedented military campaign through Asia and northeast Africa, and by the age of 30, had created one of the largest empires of the ancient world, which stretched from Greece to Egypt and into present-day Pakistan. He was undefeated in battle and is considered one of history's most successful commanders.

During his youth, Alexander was tutored by the philosopher Aristotle, until the age of 16. When he succeeded his father to the throne in 336 BCE, after Philip was assassinated, Alexander inherited a strong kingdom and an experienced army. He had been awarded the generalship of Greece and used this authority to launch his father's military expansion plans. In 334 BCE, he invaded the Achaemenid Empire, ruled Asia Minor, and began a series of campaigns that lasted ten years. Alexander broke the power of Persia in a series of decisive battles, most notably the battles of Issus and Gaugamela. He overthrew the Persian King Darius III and conquered the entirety of the Persian Empire. At that point, his empire stretched from the Adriatic Sea to the Indus River.

Seeking to reach the "ends of the world and the Great Outer Sea," he invaded India in 326 BCE but was eventually forced to turn back at the demand of his troops. Alexander died in Babylon in 323 BCE, the city he planned to establish as his capital, without executing a series of planned campaigns that would have begun with an invasion of Arabia. In the years following his death, a series of civil wars tore his empire apart, resulting in several states ruled by the Diadochi, Alexander's surviving generals and heirs. Alexander's legacy includes the cultural diffusion of his engendered conquests. He founded some 20 cities that bore his name, the most notable being Alexandria in Egypt. Alexander's settlement of Greek colonists, and the spread of Greek culture in the east resulted in a new Hellenistic civilization, aspects of which were still evident in the traditions of the Byzantine Empire in the mid-15th century. Alexander became legendary as a classical hero in the mold of Achilles, and he features prominently in the history and myth of Greek and non-Greek cultures. He became the measure against which military leaders compared themselves, and military academies throughout the world still teach his tactics.

Military Generalship

Alexander earned the honorific epithet "the Great" due to his unparalleled success as a military commander. He never lost a battle, despite typically being outnumbered. His impressive record was largely due to his smart use of terrain, phalanx and cavalry tactics, bold strategy, and the fierce loyalty of his troops. The Macedonian phalanx, armed with the sarissa, a spear up to 20 feet long, had been developed and perfected by Alexander's father, Philip II. Alexander used its speed and maneuverability to great effect against larger, but more disparate, Persian forces. Alexander also recognized the potential for disunity among his diverse army, due to the various languages, cultures, and preferred weapons individual soldiers wielded. He overcame the possibility of unrest among his troops by being personally involved in battles, as was common among Macedonian kings.

In his first battle in Asia, at Granicus, Alexander used only a small part of his forces—perhaps 13,000 infantry, with 5,000 cavalry—against a much larger Persian force of 40,000. Alexander placed the phalanx at the center, and cavalry and archers on the wings, so that his line matched the length of the Persian cavalry line. By contrast, the Persian infantry was stationed behind its cavalry. Alexander's military positioning ensured that his troops would not be outflanked; further, his phalanx, armed with long pikes, had a considerable advantage over the Persians' scimitars and javelins. Macedonian losses were negligible compared to those of the Persians.

At Issus in 333 BCE, his first confrontation with Darius, he used the same deployment, and again the central phalanx pushed through. Alexander personally led the charge in the center and routed the opposing army. At the decisive encounter with Alexander at Gaugamela, Darius equipped his chariots with scythes on the wheels to break up the phalanx and equipped his cavalry with pikes. Alexander, in turn, arranged a double phalanx, with the center advancing at an angle, which parted when the chariots bore down and reformed once they had passed. The advance proved successful and broke Darius's center, and Darius was forced to retreat once again.

Preface

For nearly two and a half thousand years, Alexander represented a central vision of mankind. His life has the flavor of a fairy story, in part because it inspired so many. Physically beautiful, a fine warrior, educated by Aristotle, born to a royal court, he chose to risk his inheritance confronting the greatest empire in Europe and Asia. He defeated the Persians in every battle and conquered their territory to the very edge of the known world. At the banks of the last river of Punjab, we are told, he wept because he had no more lands to conquer.

His soldiers, mostly older than he and desperate to return home, followed him for 10 years across 6,000 miles of Asia. In return, he was prepared to leap into their midst, unarmed, when they threatened to lynch him and to jump unsupported over the walls of Multan when they held back afraid. The empire he established over a million square miles survived in various forms for 300 years. He introduced a coinage, a legal system, a form of philosophy and a style of art that transformed culture across Asia. All this he achieved before he died at 32. His life was magnificent in scope, scale, and conviction. Ancient commentators were prepared to accept this without concealing his flaws.

Classical historians attacked him for massacring populations and destroying ancient cities; for murdering his senior staff and for leading his troops on dangerous and pointless desert crossings. Conservative Athenians saw him as a half-Barbarian, capricious Macedonian despot prone to indecent excesses of intemperance and ostentatious displays of vanity. His Macedonian followers were shocked by the respect he showed to local customs after his conquest of the Persian city of Babylon in modern Iraq. There, he took to worshipping local gods, appointed Persians to key positions, created regiments in which Asians mixed equally with Macedonians and attacked Greeks who insulted Persian custom. He was delighted, according to Arrian, when the Macedonian whom he appointed the governor of Persia "liked Oriental ways, adopted Median dress, learned the Persian language and took to living as the Persians lived". This approach was as unpopular with some Macedonian followers as it might be with some occupiers of Iraq today. But ancient writers at least had some sense of the temptations that went with being the absolute ruler of a million square miles of Asia and the most successful and wealthy man in the world before you were 30. By comparison with his drunken father, Philip, or his predecessor, the Persian king Darius, who kept 365 concubines and went to battle with a platoon of pastry chefs, Alexander seems relatively ascetic and level-headed. Most importantly, ancient writers were prepared to allow that for all his faults, Alexander was still indubitably a hero. Modern writers such as Paul Doherty take a more negative view.

Doherty introduces Alexander in The Death of a God, as a "ruthless, ambitious, self-centered prig", sketches his "deep superstition and downright cynicism" and describes, over 200 pages, his love of drink and his "paranoia and vindictiveness". He conjures up an image of a Hitler or a Stalin. Doherty describes Alexander as "a killer through and through" and says his execution of Philotas "reeks of that terror which so characterizes the great political purges of the 20th century - spies, torture... arrest at the dead of night, show trials, the lack of any appeal and immediate execution". Doherty uses this to argue that Alexander was poisoned by his companion Ptolemy. In fact, the evidence for Alexander's death is so limited that we can say little more than that he died of a fever. We have no way of telling whether the infection was the result of malaria, typhoid or a kidney stone. Paul Cartledge's account is considerably more restrained and disciplined in his use of sources, but he echoes some of Doherty's criticisms. Part of this may be a matter of Cartledge's temperament. Cartledge, an eminent Cambridge classical scholar, is particularly interested in the constitutional arrangements of the Greek states and shows little enthusiasm for warfare or the Persian world. This is unfortunate in an account of a man who was above all else a military leader and who did not return to mainland Greece after the age of 21. It makes his biography sometimes read as though it were written by one of Alexander's conservative Athenian critics - Demosthenes, for example. Cartledge argues that Alexander created a climate of fear, which provoked treachery. He emphasizes the tensions between Alexander and the Greeks and the controversy caused by Alexander's use of Persian court ceremonial and the marriage of 10,000 Macedonians to Persians at Susa. He stresses that Alexander was lucky with the timing of his Greek campaigns and with his naval policy. These are interesting claims but they are, through poor editing, repeated almost in identical words at many different points in the text.

Cartledge's book has great strengths not only in his analysis of Greek political structures but also in his illuminating and subtle account of Alexander's religious beliefs. But at times, it combines the themes of an undergraduate lecture series with the language of popular biography. Thus he describes Alexander as "Action Man incarnate", a "doer rather than a thinker", and speculates about a "repressed Oedipus complex". He tells us Alexander was "monumentally superstitious", endorses the view that he ran a "reign of terror", reminds us that "absolute power corrupts absolutely" and identifies "distinct tinges of megalomania".

It is misleading of Doherty and Cartledge to ascribe modern delusional states such as "paranoia" and "megalomania" to Alexander. It is not paranoia to suspect plots when people are trying to kill you, particularly when your father was assassinated. Many anecdotes show Alexander as trusting. Arrian reports that he was given a letter saying his doctor was about to poison him, just as the doctor had handed him a cup of medicine. Alexander passed the letter to the doctor and drank the potion before the doctor had time to read the letter. It is not megalomania to imagine yourself a world-historical figure of unparalleled wealth, power and success when you are.

Curiously, it is a coffee table book with few academic pretensions, which seems most comfortable balancing Alexander's crimes with his greatness. Laura Foreman's Alexander the Conqueror is a good example of popular history. It is excellently illustrated, including photographs from modern Turkey, Syria, and Afghanistan, and even a picture of the remote oasis of Siwah in Libya where Alexander led a near-disastrous desert pilgrimage. She writes well and the editing is good (though not flawless - she is wrong about the site of Ecbatana). She finds his deeds appalling but she concedes that these were "if not survival traits, at least requisites for extraordinary accomplishment". Ultimately, however, she describes him as "perfidious, devious, cruel and murderous, willing to sacrifice anything on the altar of his unquenchable lust for glory".

Doherty, Cartledge, and Foreman, like many modern writers, find it difficult to forgive Alexander's ambition. They see such ambition as a weakness in his claim to be a true Hellenic hero. Cartledge writes that Alexander would not allow his promotion of Hellenic culture to get in the way of his "one overriding ideal, the power and glory of Alexander". But few classical critics would have drawn such a distinction. They grasped that Alexander's love of glory was a reflection of his Hellenic background and an essential component of his heroism. His glory lay in personifying the highest virtues of Homeric culture. He wanted to be regarded as the epitome of his tutor Aristotle's virtuous man: generous, brave in war and great in soul, magnificent in gesture, proud and obsessed with honor. But most of all he wanted to be Achilles and that meant wanting, in his favorite words from Achilles, to be "the best, the best among the best: now and in perpetuity". Achilles, like Alexander, aimed not to be simply the fastest runner, though he was quick, nor a successful warrior, though he fought well. He wished to be acknowledged absolutely as our superior not just in the body or in mind but in the very essence of his character. He tried to live like a god.

Alexander quite consciously aimed to be a hero imitated other heroes and promoted himself as a hero. This underlay the scale of his achievements, the extremity of his courage and his charisma. And such ambition could be seen as a form of insecurity. Certainly, because he was not a god but only playing one, there was a gap between the real Alexander and his image as a hero, which could only be bridged by role-playing, exaggeration, and rhetoric and by a culture which tolerated this kind of self-projection.

His contemporaries, and indeed audiences as late as the 19th century, saw nothing inconsistent in the coexistence of self-promotion, fantasy and greatness. They were prepared to allow that real merit could coexist with dreams and showmanship.

We are no longer prepared to accept this. Competitiveness, egotism, self-promotion, and rhetoric are seen as weaknesses. Concepts of honor, nobility, and magnificence, appropriate to male, aristocratic warriors, seem ridiculous and irrelevant. Our values are now too diverse for us to agree on who might be "the best of men". We are not prepared to acknowledge other men as "great" or our moral superiors. There are now more famous people than ever: some are famous for their plastic surgery or their skill with their right foot, some are famous for nothing in particular. We write about them with an easy familiarity, focusing on their flaws and ordinariness. Modern celebrities are not terrifying exemplars and we do not credit them with honor, nobility or greatness of soul. We acknowledge self-sacrificing heroes such as the 9/11 firemen but we emphasize their modesty. We like our heroes to be accidental heroes. We can no longer accept or create the conditions of Alexander's heroism.

Only a curiously antique historical novel by Stephen Pressfield captures something of Alexander's glamour and appeal. A close study of pre-modern battles has allowed him to evoke with precision and plausibility the experience of a classical cavalry charge. He emphasizes the risk Alexander took in leading an army of 40,000 against the Persian king on his home ground. Darius had been training between a quarter of a million and a million men on the plains outside Babylon for 18 months, having even gone so far as to manicure the ground like a putting green for his scythed chariots. His battle line must have overlapped Alexander's by hundreds of yards on either side, making it easy for him to envelop both wings.

Pressfield brilliantly illustrates Arrian's description of Alexander's successful strategy, which was to draw off

Darius's cavalry at an oblique angle and then concentrate his forces in a single wedge, charging straight at the Persian king. And he expands convincingly on the charisma Alexander must have exerted to persuade his troops to follow him against such odds. But even Pressman does not entirely escape modern, anachronistic perspectives on Alexander. His description of Alexander's campaigns in the Hindu Kush reads too much like a documentary on Taliban guerrillas and he does not attempt to explore what it meant for Alexander to take seriously the idea that he was a god. Outside the pages of historical romance, it seems the old heroes are dead. We don't permit them to exist. We tend to agree with a more recent global hero, Charlie Chaplin, who wrote: "I'm sorry, but I don't want to be emperor. I don't want to rule or conquer anyone."

This is in some ways a tribute to the maturity in our society. The classical hero was driven, from an early age, by a false and lonely conception of himself. Alexander strove to forge an image and attract worshippers. He was haunted by the competition of dead men and the need to out-do everyone who had ever lived. He was half-aware that his own greatness was partly an act and he gave his life with a social fiction called "honor" for a fantasy called "heroism". To move beyond this is partial enlightenment. Yet what is its replacement? The old idea gave a purpose and possibility to human life - it celebrated humanity through the idea of super-humans. We are all now reduced to the last moments of Don Quixote. We still fantasize about heroes like Alexander but when we try to realize our fantasies, we do so half-heartedly - pursuing an idea which we suspect is not only impossible but also ridiculous.

PART 1

CHAPTER 1

Who was Alexander the Great and what he did?

Alexander was the third King of Macedon and can be regarded as one of the best military personnel the world has ever seen. His military genius brought him tremendous success and managed to stretch the Empire of Macedon from Greece to India. Alexander the Great, as he is known today, is credited with conquering and annexing to his glorious empire nearly half of the world's population during his time.

Tremendously successful in all military coups, Alexander the Great spread the Greek civilization all over the East, till the borders of India, and changed the course of history until he died at the age of 33. In his short life, he managed so many things as to become a legend.

The First Years

Alexander was born in 356 BC in Pella, the capital of the Macedon Kingdom. His father was King Phillip II of Macedon and his mother was Olympias, the daughter of the king of Epirus. The two of them had met in Samothraki island during some religious festivals and, although Phillip also had other wives, Olympias was thought as his primary wife and queen. The myth says that the night Alexander was born, the temple of Artemis in Ephesus, one of the Seven Wonders of the World, was burnt down as the goddess was not there to protect it, being busy to attend the birth of that boy who would later become a legend.

Since he was a little boy, Alexander was taught by the best tutors and had shown special courage in fights. At the age of 10, to everyone's surprise, he managed to tame a very wild horse. Since then, this horse which was named Bucephalus became his companion in all battles and wars.

When Alexander was 13, he came under the tutelage of Aristotle, the famous philosopher. Aristotle taught some very important and interesting subjects to him and his courses covered topics on biology, philosophy, religion, logic, and art. During this learning process, Alexander developed favoritism for Homer's literature, especially the epic of Iliad, and became a great fun of Achilles, whom he had as his exemplar.

Ancient sources state Alexander to be short, much shorter than a normal Macedonian, but very tough. His beard was scanty and it is reported that he had a short of spinal problem: his neck was twisted and some believe that he had a congenital spinal disorder.

At 16, when he finished his education, he was constantly involved in fights against the tribe of the Illyrians, who threatened the Macedonian Empire. Along with his father, he participated in the Battle of Chaeronea in 338 BC and defeated both Athenians and Thebans who had formed an alliance against Macedonia. Together they occupied Central Greece and then marched to Peloponnese. There at Corinth, that Philip got the recognition of Supreme Commander of all Greeks in the war they wanted to launch against Persia.

When King Phillip II returned to his kingdom, he was charmed by a Macedonian noblewoman Cleopatra Eurydice, whom he married soon. Their marriage bore doubts in the minds of many as because their offspring would be true Macedonian blood and a possible heir to the throne. Such thoughts were even spoken aloud in the banquet ceremony before the wedding, which led to a heated exchange of words and actions between Alexander and his father.

Next day, the day of his wedding to Cleopatra, King Phillip was assassinated by Pausanias, his chief bodyguard, for unknown reasons. Some said that it was Olympias who had ordered the assassination of her husband from jealousy. Others believed that the Persians had arranged everything to prevent a war against them, while Alexander himself was also suspect as he faced the danger not to become king, after the birth of Cleopatra's son.

The result was that at the early age of 20, Alexander the great had to take his father's position on the throne. Soon regions of Thebes, Athens, Thessaly, and the Thracian tribes revolted against Macedon to acquire their independence now that Phillip was dead. Alexander got the news very quickly and he acted spontaneously. He first crushed the Thessalian forces making them surrender and went south to face other battles.

In Corinth, he met the Athenians who opted for peace and persuaded all the Greeks to make his father's dream true: to start the war against the Persians in order first to take revenge for the Persian Wars, about a century earlier, and then to minimize the risk of a new Persian attack.

Conquering the East

It was in the springtime of 334 BC that Alexander the Great set out to conquer Persia with an army of soldiers from all Greek towns, except Sparta that denied taking part in this war. The generals of his army were all Macedonians. They were Antigonus, Ptolemy, and Seleucus. In the ancient city of Troy, close to the River Granicus, the Macedonian army defeated the Persian forces and occupied all the coastline of Asia Minor. While in Troy, the myth says that Alexander paid tributes to the grave of Achilles, his eternal model.

At the Battle of Issus, in 333 BC, the Macedonian army for the first time came face to face with the real Persian army led by King Darius III. Darius was defeated and he succumbed to Alexander, who proclaimed himself to be the King of Asia. Alexander moved then to Egypt, where he was viewed upon as a liberator to free Egypt from the Persians. There he was named Pharaoh and established the city of Alexandria, that exists and flourishes till today. Alexander went on to the west to occupy Babylon, the capital of the Persian Empire.

In Babylon, he resided in the Palace of Darius and married his daughter, princess Statira. The ambitions of Alexander brought his army to modern Afghanistan and Pakistan, where he married the daughter of a local leader, Roxana. This was rather a strange decision and raised many reactions from his general, but Alexander considered it a symbolic action: a Greek king married a local princess and population's of the West and the East could finally unite into one empire, as was his dream.

In the meantime, the relationship of Alexander with his generals was getting bad. After some conspiracies against his life, Alexander didn't trust them any more except for one general, Hephaestion, the son of a Macedon nobleman and long friend of his. The Macedon generals would also protest against some Persian traditions and practices that Alexander demanded from them, such as the custom of kneeling before him. This was a natural practice for the Persians to show their respect to the king but the Greeks kneeled only before the statues of the gods, not to their kings, so the generals considered it as an act of indignity to kneel in front of a man.

After long years of marching and fighting, Alexander the Great had yet reached the borders of India but fighting with the local tribes was very difficult. In fact, in a battle, Alexander lost his beloved horse, Bucephalus. Plus his army was much tired from so many years of wars and they wanted to rest. That is when Alexander decided to return to Babylon for a few months and then come back to conquer India.

Biographical aspects of his life, early life, and so on

He was born in 356 BCE at Pella in Macedonia, the son of Philip II and Olympias (daughter of King Neoptolemus of Epirus). From age 13 to 16 he was taught by Aristotle, who inspired him with an interest in philosophy, medicine, and scientific investigation, but he was later to advance beyond his teacher's narrow precept that non-Greeks should be treated as slaves. Left in charge of Macedonia in 340 during Philip's attack on Byzantium, Alexander defeated the Maedi, a Thracian people. Two years later he commanded the left wing at the Battle of Chaeronea, in which Philip defeated the allied Greek states, and displayed personal courage in breaking the Sacred Band of Thebes, an elite military corps composed of 150 pairs of lovers. A year later Philip divorced Olympias, and, after a quarrel at a feast held to celebrate his father's new marriage, Alexander and his mother fled to Epirus, and Alexander later went to Illyria. Shortly afterward, father and son were reconciled and Alexander returned, but his position as heir was jeopardized.

In 336, however, on Philip's assassination, Alexander, acclaimed by the army, succeeded without opposition. He at once executed the princes of Lyncestis, alleged to be behind Philip's murder, along with all possible rivals and the whole of the faction opposed to him. He then marched south, recovered a wavering Thessaly, and at an assembly of the Greek League of Corinth was appointed generalissimo for the forthcoming invasion of Asia, already planned and initiated by Philip. Returning to Macedonia by way of Delphi (where the Pythian priestess acclaimed him "invincible"), he advanced into Thrace in spring 335 and, after forcing the Shipka Pass and crushing the Triballi, crossed the Danube to disperse the Getae; turning west, he then defeated and shattered a coalition of Illyrians who had invaded Macedonia. Meanwhile, a rumor of his death had precipitated a revolt of Theban democrats; other Greek states favored Thebes, and the Athenians, urged on by Demosthenes, voted help. In 14 days Alexander marched 240 miles from Pelion (near modern Korçë, Albania) in Illyria to Thebes. When the Thebans refused to surrender, he made an entry and razed their city to the ground, sparing only temples and Pindar's house; 6,000 were killed and all survivors sold into slavery. The other Greek states were cowed by this severity, and Alexander could afford to treat Athens leniently. Macedonian garrisons were left in Corinth, Chalcis, and the Cadmea (the citadel of Thebes).

CHAPTER 2

Becoming Alexander the Great

Alexander the Great, born in 356 BCE in Pella, Macedonia, was the son of Philip of Macedon and Princess Olympias of Epirus. As a young boy he was always fearless, strong, and eager to learn. He went on to inherit each of his parents best qualities. His father was an excellent general and organizer, while his mother was extremely intelligent. At the age of thirteen, he became a pupil of Aristotle. It was Aristotle who inspired Alexander's great love for literature. Through his mentor, Alexander learned the Greek ways of living and the ideals of Greek civilization. However, it was not all work and no play for the young Alexander. He spent a great deal of time participating in sports and daily exercise to develop a strong body.

At a fairly young age, Alexander was given many responsibilities. His father made him his ambassador to Athens when he was eighteen. Two years later he became the King of Macedonia. During this time the Greek states had become restless under Macedonian rule. While Alexander was away fighting, the people of Thebes seized the opportunity and revolted. When Alexander returned he attacked the city and destroyed almost everything in sight. This dissipated any further attempts at rebellion and Alexander quickly united the Greek cities and formed the League of Nations, of which he became president.

Soon after this victory, Alexander set out to conquer Persia. On the banks of the Granicus River Alexander quickly defeated the Persian troops who had been waiting for him. This victory made the rest of Asia Minor vulnerable. In 333 BCE Alexander marched into Syria. Even though Darius III, King of Persia, had raised a large army he was unable to withstand Alexander's powerful infantry and phalanx. The entire region soon submitted to Alexander. Following this, he went to Egypt, where he was welcomed as a deliverer because the Egyptians hated their cruel Persian rulers. It was here that Alexander founded the famous city that bears his name. Alexandria, situated on a strip of land between Lake Mareotis and the Mediterranean Sea, became a world center of commerce and learning.

Alexander was soon drawn into battle with the Persians again. In the decisive Battle of Gaugamela, Alexander routed Darius and forced his entire army east. After this, the city of Babylon surrendered, which allowed Alexander to easily capture Susa and Persepolis. Darius was soon killed by one of his generals which made Alexander King of Asia. He did not rest for long, as he had set his sights on India. In 326 BCE Alexander defeated Porus, the prince of India.

Alexander was now at the height of his power. His empire stretched from the Ionian Sea to northern India. However, Alexander had even greater plans. He wanted to combine Asia and Europe into one country, and named Babylon the new capital. In order to attain this goal, he encouraged intermarriages, did away with corrupt officials, and spread Greek ideas, customs, and laws into Asia. The great and many plans that he had abruptly came to an end. While in Babylon Alexander became seriously ill with malaria and on June 13, 323 BCE he died. During his time he conquered most of the civilized world and has been remembered as one of the greatest generals in history.

Alexander The Great's Education and Beginnings

He was born in 356 BCE at Pella in Macedonia, the son of Philip II and Olympias (daughter of King Neoptolemus of Epirus). From age 13 to 16 he was taught by Aristotle, who inspired him with an interest in philosophy, medicine, and scientific investigation, but he was later to advance beyond his teacher's narrow precept that non-Greeks should be treated as slaves. Left in charge of Macedonia in 340 during Philip's attack on Byzantium, Alexander defeated the Maedi, a Thracian people. Two years later he commanded the left wing at the Battle of Chaeronea, in which Philip defeated the allied Greek states, and displayed personal courage in breaking the Sacred Band of Thebes, an elite military corps composed of 150 pairs of lovers.

From an early age, Alexander displayed the tremendous military talent and was appointed as a commander in his father's army at the age of 18. Having conquered all of Greece, Phillip was about to embark on a campaign to invade Greece's arch-enemy, the Persian Empire. Before he could invade Persia, Phillip was assassinated, possibly by Alexander, who then became king in 336BCE. Two years later in 334 BCE, he crossed the Hellespont (in modern-day Turkey) with 45,000 men and invaded the Persian Empire.

In three colossal battles – Granicus, Issus and Gaugamela – that took place between 334 and 331, Alexander brilliantly (and often recklessly) led his army to victory against Persian armies that may have outnumbered his own as much as ten to one. By 331 BCE, the Persian Empire was defeated, the Persian Emperor Darius was dead, and Alexander was the undisputed ruler of the Mediterranean. His military campaign lasted 12 years and took him and his army 10,000 miles to the Indus River in India.

Only the weariness of his men and Alexander's untimely death in 323BCE at the age of 32 ended the Greek conquest of the known world. It is said that when Alexander looked at his empire, he wept for there was nothing more to conquer. His vast empire did not survive his death but fragmented into three large chunks centered in Greece, Egypt, and Syria and controlled by his former generals.

At its largest, Alexander's empire stretched from Egypt to India. He built six Greek cities, all named Alexandria. (Only Alexandria in Egypt still survives) These cities, and the Greeks who settled in them, brought Greek culture to the center of the oldest civilizations of Mesopotamia.

CHAPTER 3

Philosophy about and War

Classical Greek philosophy is that portion of Ancient Western philosophy that begins with the end of the war against Persia in 479BC and ends with the deaths of Aristotle and Alexander the Great in 322BC. The previous period of philosophy is called Pre-Socratic, not because the philosophers all died before Socrates did philosophy, but because they were not influenced by Socrates and did not answer to his thought. The next period of philosophy is called Hellenistic, not because the Greeks previously did no philosophy, but because the efforts of Alexander the Great changed everything. Classical philosophy is focused on the philosophy of Socrates, those influenced by him and the philosophy produced by those people prior to Alexander the Great. There are a number of philosophical schools started in this time, as well as a number of famous philosophers.

In context, this was a history of relative freedom, especially in Athens, even while war happened on again and off again. During this period, the first historians appeared. Herodotus (484-425BC) was the first historian and the first to mention contact with India. Thucydides (460-395BC) was the first historian to promote something like the modern historical method. He wrote about the wars between Athens and Sparta. It was also during this period that a number of dramatist's appeared, including Aristophanes who ridiculed Socrates in his play "Clouds". Finally, this period was a period of scientific discovery. There was no distinction between philosophy and science, so these scientists are counted as philosophers during this time period. It was during this period that Hippocrates (460-370BC) established medicine as a discipline distinct from philosophy. Many discoveries were made in astronomy, mathematics, biology, and geology.

Philosophically, the Classical period was one in which philosophy was establishing the very first schools of thought and learning to interact with previous philosophers. Most philosophers learned from a single teacher who would teach them everything they knew about philosophy. Like the previous period in philosophy, a lot of philosophers either did not write anything or their writings are now lost. Unlike that period, the writings of some philosophers are still around today. The range of opinions started at this time or continued from the previous period encompass almost every possible philosophical opinion imaginable. It was because of this that philosophers began to interact with previous philosophers.

Socrates, Plato, and Aristotle are the most important philosophers of this time period. However, various other philosophers and philosophical schools are important. Antisthenes became the first Cynic. He believed in the pursuit of virtue against pleasure. Epicurus started the popular school of philosophy after his own name. He believed in the pursuit of pleasure. These philosophers and their schools either contributed to the development of later philosophy or were important in their own time.

Greek philosophers were edging towards the radical idea that there were no gods who controlled the destiny of life on earth from some detached mountaintop. Rather, it was the man himself who, thanks to his own brainpower, could decipher the laws of the universe to become master of all nature. Supreme among such thinkers as Aristotle (384BCE-322BCE). The scope of his works was truly immense, covering everything from speculations on the nature of the human soul to the physics of the universe; from city politics and personal ethics to the history of plants and animals; and from public speaking and poetry to music, memory, and logic.

Aristotle combined what he considered the best of what he had learned from his teacher, Plato, and other Greek philosophers such as Thales, with everything he observed in the natural world. It led him to a single, profound conclusion: underneath all reality, there was indeed a fundamental set of universal natural laws that explained everything to do with life, the universe and everything from human politics to the weather. To understand these rules of nature was to understand reality. The key was a careful observation of the universe and its systems by good use of the human senses and then, by using human reason and intellect, to uncover the truth.

The question that Aristotle's scientific, rational view of the world provoked was this: in a mechanistic universe governed by rules, what place was there for old-fashioned, whimsical gods? His answer was simple. It was the rules of nature themselves that were the very essence of all that is divine in the universe: "For God is to us a law, impartial, admitting not to correction or change, and better I think and surer than those which are engraved upon tablets," he said.

Aristotle gave mankind the confidence to explore, discover and learn. But such insights would be useless hidden in the mind of one brilliant man, or stored in a rich patron's library. To fulfill their potential, these ideas needed a force to scatter them far and wide, giving as many human cultures as possible the chance to exert the power of human brains over nature's brawn.

As luck would have it, Aristotle's pupil, the young Prince Alexander of Macedon, was just the right man at just the right time. Quite possibly it was his great teacher's passion for the natural world that fired Alexander, impregnating him with a feverish determination to see everything in the world for himself, conquering whatever empires lay en route.

Alexander ascended to the throne of Macedonia in North Greece at the age of just 20, in 336BCE. For the next 13 years, Alexander led an army of 42,000 Greek soldiers on an extraordinary military adventure across Persia, Egypt and even into India. On his way, he famously "undid" the impossible-to-untie Gordian knot by slashing it with his sword, and he routed the Persian Emperor Darius III at the Battle of Issus in 333BCE. He then marched down the Mediterranean coast, laying siege to the city of Tyre, which he eventually took after seven months, clearing the way towards Egypt, where, thanks to the decline of Persian power, he was welcomed as a liberator and pronounced Pharaoh in 332BCE. Here, Alexander founded the most famous of all the cities named after him, Alexandria, establishing it as the main seaport linking Egypt with Greece, the maritime axis of a new and increasingly powerful Hellenic empire.

Eighteen months later, Alexander left Egypt, marching back to Persia, where again he defeated Darius at the Battle of Gaugamela. This time the Persian king fled from the battlefield only to be murdered by his own troops in the mountains of Media. The way was now open for Alexander to conquer all Persia, first marching on Babylon, then Susa, the ancient Assyrian capital, and finally Persepolis, the magnificent royal home of the Persian kings.

With the death of Darius and the submission of Egypt and Persia, Alexander's military goals had been accomplished. But still, the warrior in him could not be controlled. Having sent many of his Greek soldiers back home, he now paid mercenaries to fight for him in a new imperial army and set off on a three-year campaign to subjugate Scythia and Afghanistan before reaching the River Indus in northern India.

Despite Alexander's determination to cross the sacred River Ganges and march into the heart of India, his men had reached their limit. Eventually, Alexander and a company of soldiers made their way back to Persia across deserts and plains. On the afternoon of 10 June 323BCE, in the palace of Nebuchadnezzar II in Babylon, Alexander died, probably of malaria. He was one month short of his 33rd birthday.

Many historians have devoted their professional lives to the study of this man, yet no one really knows what drove him to try to conquer the world. Whatever his motivation, the result of his conquests caused the Greek language to become the lingua franca across the entire Middle East and Egypt. Thousands of Greek people, some soldiers, others merchants, artisans, scientists, and philosophers, moved abroad, taking with them their experimental world views. Of the seven wonders of the ancient world, five were Greek constructions – each one an awesome monument to these people's confidence in mankind's power over the natural world.

Roman love for all things Greek was particularly focused around the personality and career of Alexander, who after his death became antiquity's greatest role model. Roman emperors came to regard Alexander as the epitome of leadership, strength, and courage.

PART 2
CHAPTER 4

King of Macedon

The accomplishments of both King Philip II and his son, Alexander the Great are amongst the most celebrated and controversial of Ancient Greece. No matter how you view what they did, they couldn't have done it without their army. The army was formed by King Philip and then the tradition continued with Alexander. In fact, the Macedonian army began in 357 BC when Philip II became the king and then ended with the death of Alexander the Great in 323 BC.

Here's more information:

The Formation of the Army and the Reign of Philip II

The unification of the Ancient Macedonia Army occurred within a year of Philip II's ascendancy to the throne, after the death of his elder brothers, King Alexander II and Perdiccas III. Philip II desired to unify Macedon itself through the formation of strong, order army which became Macedon's greatest source of wealth. Philip II achieved this in part by greatly increasing the number of troops in the army and made it the source of its wealth and power. Philip also increased the speed of the Macedonian Army by ridding it of wheeled transport and lowering the number of servants which would travel with the army. This allowed the army to diligently progress across the areas surrounding Macedon.

The Structure of the Macedonian Army

The Macedonian army was greatly distinguished by its Companion Cavalry, seen by many historians as the greatest cavalry in antiquity. This cavalry was divided into sub-units of 200 men each with the exception of the leading squadron, the Royal Squadron, which had 300 men. The Macedonian Army utilized a "wedge" formation with its cavalry. this formation is a triangular-shaped configuration which the cavalry formed into as it went into battle.

Philip II also introduced catapults into his army, one of the first leaders in history to do so. Within one year of Philip II's leading the army, the Macedonians had reclaimed the territory known as Upper Macedonia, which had been taken from Macedon by the neighboring Illyrians, who inhabited the Balkans. The army that Philip II formed was not merely of Macedonians but also of inhabitants of neighboring areas. From the north of Macedon came skirmishers, who were helpful in bombarding the enemy and committing uphill attacks. Mercenary troops of conquered territories were also incorporated into Philip's Army.

The Army and Alexander the Great

After Philip was assassinated Alexander the Great took the throne. He was only 20 years old. Under the leadership of Alexander, the Macedonian Army was able to defeat the Persian empire and expand Greek settlements farther East than Greece had ever been able to before. This helped to spread Greek culture into Greek Asia, a phenomenon we now refer to as Hellenization. As a leader, Alexander the Great strengthened the Macedonian army with his brilliant strategic skills. He also improved the cavalry and incorporated allied forces in the Macedonian Army.

The ancient kingdom of Macedon, which Alexander inherited after the assassination of his father, Philip II, in

336 BC, largely coincides with the region of Northern Greece that is now called Makedonia or Macedonia. It is here that Alexander was born, spent the formative years of his childhood and youth, and gained his first experiences as a military and political leader.

The origins of Macedon are somewhat hazy, as the kingdom becomes historically visible in the 8th or 7th century BC, but remained a bit of a backwater throughout the 6th and 5th centuries, the era of the great Greek city-states further south. For a short period around the Second Persian War, King Alexander I (Alexander the Great is actually Alexander III, his great-great-great-grandson), even had to accept the Persian Empire as his overlord.

The meteoric rise of Macedon is associated especially with Philip II. This gifted leader used his rule (359-336 BC) to first unite the kingdom and limit the powers of the local nobilities in its various centers. Next, he engaged in a whole series of military campaigns to expand its borders considerably in all directions, including the conquest of most of Thessaly to the South. Eventually, he took on the great city-states of the southern mainland, culminating in his resounding defeat of the armies of Athens and Thebes at the 338 BC Battle of Chaironeia (his cavalry was then commanded by the 18-year-old Alexander), which established Macedon as the hegemonic power dominating Greece. Philip's achievements were the basis that enabled Alexander to take on the Persians soon after becoming king, setting out from Macedon on his long campaign, never to return to his homeland.

After Alexander's conquests, his early death and the break-up of his empire, Macedon remained the dominant power in Greece for another century-and-a-half, ending with its final defeat by Rome at the Battle of Pydna in 168 BC.

The Greek region of Macedonia contains countless sites and museums standing witness to the golden age of ancient Macedon, many of which are intimately connected to the lives of Philip II and Alexander the Great. They are one of the key foci of our Exploring Macedonia tour, a 14-day trip we have carefully designed to present the beauties and historical riches of that fascinating and highly diverse area, ranging from prehistory to the modern period and guided by two archaeologists.

One of the must-see sites is Pella, Alexander's birthplace. Founded by King Archelaos in 399 BC, Pella was to remain the (main) capital of the kingdom of Macedon until its destruction and sack by the Romans. Greek archaeologists have revealed the sprawling remains of a huge Hellenistic city, including public buildings such as various temples and a vast agora or marketplace, as well as the foundations of extremely grand private homes, their floors decorated with wonderful pebble mosaics. The new archaeological museum of Pella houses an astonishing collection of high-quality objects from the settlement itself and from its surrounding cemeteries, a treasure trove of Hellenistic art, but also of objects representing daily life in antiquity.

Further west, we visit Mieza, set in the lovely hill country near Naousa, now famous as the heart of one of Macedonia's most famous wine regions (needless to say, we will sample its produce). A leafy glade is the location of the ancient nymphaeum or shrine of the nymphs. It was here that Aristotle, the greatest philosopher of his age and one of the founder heroes of Western thought, tutored Alexander the Great and his companions between 343 and 340 BC when the young prince was aged 13 to 16. It is a place of intense charm and serene atmosphere, in an area scattered with Macedonian tombs. Not far to the north of Mieza is Edessa. Although most of the archaeological remains there are of Roman date, recent excavations have also revealed part of the 4th century BC fortification of its hilltop acropolis, probably built by order of Philip II himself. They are preserved under a glass floor in a beautiful 19th-century mansion - which happens to be the hotel we stay in!

Conquest of the Persian Empire

Alexander III the Great, the King of Macedonia and conqueror of the Persian Empire is considered one of the greatest military geniuses of all times. He was an inspiration for later conquerors such as Hannibal the Carthaginian, the Romans Pompey and Caesar, and Napoleon. Alexander was born in 356 BC in Pella, the ancient capital of Macedonia. He was a son of Philip II, King of Macedonia, and Olympias, the princess of neighboring Epirus.

Alexander spent his childhood watching his father transforming Macedonia into a great military power, winning victory after victory on the battlefields throughout the Balkans. At age 12 he showed his equestrian skill to his father and all who were watching when he tamed Bucephalus, an unruly stallion horse, unable to be ridden and devouring the flesh of all who had tried. Plutarch writes: "Philip and his friends looked on at first in silence and anxiety for the result, till seeing him turn at the end of his career, and come back rejoicing and triumphing for what he had performed, they all burst out into acclamations of applause; and his father shedding tears, it is said, for joy, kissed him as he came down from his horse, and in his transport said, 'O my son, look thee out a kingdom equal to and worthy of thyself, for Macedonia is too little for thee' " (Alex. 6.8.).

Alexander would ride Bucephalus in all of his major battles, together till the very end. When he was 13, Philip hired the Greek philosopher Aristotle to be Alexander's personal tutor. During the next three years, Aristotle gave Alexander training in rhetoric and literature and stimulated his interest in science, medicine, and philosophy, all of which became of importance in Alexander's later life.

In 340, when Philip assembled a large Macedonian army and invaded Thrace, he left his 16 years old son with the power to rule Macedonia in his absence as regent, which shows that even at such young age Alexander was recognized as quite capable. But as the Macedonian army advanced deep into Thrace, the Thracian tribe of Maedi bordering north-eastern Macedonia rebelled and posed a danger to the country. Alexander assembled an army, led it against the rebels, and with swift action defeated the Maedi, captured their stronghold, and renamed it after himself to Alexandroupolis. Two years later in 338 BC, Philip gave his son a commanding post among the senior generals as the Macedonian army invaded Greece. At the Battle of Chaeronea, the Greeks were defeated and Alexander displayed his bravery by destroying the elite Greek force, the Theban Secret Band. Some ancient historians recorded that the Macedonians won the battle thanks to his bravery.

Alexander's army crossed the Hellespont with about 40,000 Greek soldiers. After an initial victory against Persian forces at the Battle of the Granicus, Alexander accepted the surrender of the Persian provincial capital and treasury of Sardis and proceeded down the Ionian coast. At Halicarnassus, Alexander successfully waged the first of many sieges, eventually forcing his opponents, the mercenary captain Memnon of Rhodes and the Persian satrap of Caria, Orontobates, to withdraw by sea. Alexander left Caria in the hands of Ada of Caria, the sister of Mausolus, whom Orontobates had deposed. From Halicarnassus, Alexander proceeded into mountainous Lycia and the Pamphylian plain, asserting control over all coastal cities and denying them to his enemy. From Pamphylia onwards the coast held no major ports, so Alexander moved inland. At Termessus Alexander humbled but did not storm the Pisidian city. At the ancient Phrygian capital of Gordium, Alexander "undid" the tangled Gordian knot, a feat said to await the future "king of Asia." According to the most vivid story, Alexander proclaimed that it did not matter how the knot was undone and hacked it apart with his sword. Another version claims that he did not use the sword but actually figured out how to undo the knot. It is difficult, perhaps impossible, to decide which story is correct.

Alexander's army crossed the Cilician Gates and met and defeated the main Persian army under the command of Darius III at the Battle of Issus in 333 B.C.E. Darius fled this battle in such a panic for his life that he left behind his wife, his children, his mother, and much of his personal treasure. Sisygambis, the queen-mother, never forgave Darius for abandoning her. She disowned him and adopted Alexander as her son instead. Proceeding down the Mediterranean coast, he took Tyre and Gaza after famous sieges. Alexander passed near but probably did not visit Jerusalem.

In 332-331 B.C.E., Alexander was welcomed as a liberator in Egypt and was pronounced the son of Zeus by Egyptian priests of the god Ammon at the oracle of Ammon located at the Siwa Oasis in the Libyan Desert. He founded Alexandria in Egypt, which would become the prosperous capital of the Ptolemaic Dynasty after his death. Leaving Egypt, Alexander marched eastward into Assyria (now Iraq) and defeated Darius and a third Persian army at the Battle of Gaugamela. Darius was forced to flee the field after his charioteer was killed, and Alexander chased him as far as Arbela. While Darius fled over the mountains to Ecbatana (modern Hamadan), Alexander marched to Babylon.

From Babylon, Alexander went to Susa, one of the Achaemenid capitals, and captured its treasury. Sending the bulk of his army to Persepolis, the Persian capital, by the Royal Road, Alexander stormed and captured the Persian Gates (in the modern Zagros Mountains), then sprinted for Persepolis before its treasury could be looted. Alexander allowed the League forces to loot Persepolis, and he set fire to the royal palace of Xerxes, allegedly in revenge for the burning of the Athenian Acropolis during the Greco-Persian Wars. He then set off in pursuit of Darius, who was kidnapped and then murdered by followers of Bessus, his Bactrian satrap and kinsman. Bessus then declared himself Darius' successor as Artaxerxes V and retreated into Central Asia to launch a guerrilla campaign against Alexander. With the death of Darius, Alexander declared the war of vengeance at an end and released his Greek and other allies from service in the League campaign (although he allowed those that wished to re-enlist as mercenaries in his imperial army). His three-year campaign against Bessus and his successor Spitamenes took him through Medes, Parthia, Aria, Drangiana, Arachosia, Bactria, and Scythia. In the process, he captured and re-founded Herat and Samarkand, and he founded a series of new cities, all called Alexandria, including one near modern Kandahar in Afghanistan, and Alexandria Eschate ("The Furthest") bordering today's Chinese Turkestan.

The four great battles Alexander fought in the course of his brilliant military career, the Battle of the Granicus, fought in May 334 BC, was the first–and the one in which he came closest to failure and death. The Granicus is also worthy of note because it is one of the earliest battles on record that was decided largely by cavalry strength, though coordinated with infantry support. Although some of the tactical details of the fighting are reasonably clear, to this day one of the more puzzling aspects is Alexander's strategy of opening the battle with a feint attack. Unfortunately, the three major ancient literary sources–Arrian, Diodorus, and Plutarch–give very little real detail of the battle, focusing rather on Alexander's heroic struggle. Nevertheless, by carefully reviewing those literary sources, a highly probable picture of the battle emerges.

After the death of his father, King Philip II, in 336 BC, Alexander III won the allegiance of the army and ascended to the throne of Macedon at age 20, only to find himself at the head of a rebellious kingdom. The sudden death of his father had encouraged the barbarians to the north and west–and several Greek cities to the south–to revolt against Macedonian rule. Within two years, Alexander had suppressed all internal opposition, crushed the barbarian revolts indecisive campaigns and subdued the Greek insurrection. Once he had consolidated his power at home, Alexander enthusiastically took on the project his father had planned but never carried out–an invasion of the Persian Empire.

For well over a century, the Persians' increasing interference in Greek mainland affairs, their oppression of Greek coastal cities in western Asia Minor and their repeated invasions of Greece had filled the Greeks with fear and loathing. In the spring of 334 BC, Alexander led a combined Macedonian, Greek and Balkan (historically referred to as Macedonian) army of 32,000 infantry and 5,100 cavalries on a 20-day march from Macedon to the Hellespont (today called the Dardanelles). Alexander knew that agents sent by King Darius III of Persia had had much to do with inciting the Greeks against him. To his personal desire for revenge, he now harnessed to his cause the Greeks' grievances over Persian injustices done to them, past and present.

Prior to Alexander's Hellespont crossing, the Persian satraps (provincial governors) and others in the Persian high command assembled their forces of about 10,000 cavalries and 5,000 infantry near the town of Zelea in western Asia Minor (present-day Turkey). A council of war–to which Memnon, a high-ranking Greek mercenary in Persian service, was admitted–was held to discuss strategy. Knowing that the Macedonian army would be a formidable adversary, Memnon advised the Persians to burn crops, farms, and villages in the country through which Alexander would have to pass, thereby depriving him of provisions, while the Persian army withdrew eastward and avoided battle. The satraps, however, distrusted Memnon because he was a Greek, and they were reluctant to see their territories destroyed. Consequently, they rejected his sound advice and decided to stay to defend their provinces.

The Persian nobles believed themselves superior to the barbaric invaders and counted on a full array of western satraps, a numerically superior cavalry (which for generations was reputed to be the finest in existence), a formidable contingent of Greek mercenary infantry and a sound plan to stop the invasion at the onset. They seem to have had two major objectives. First, they would strategically force Alexander toward a carefully chosen position before he could move farther inland; if he did not move toward that position, he would leave his rear unprotected and possibly lose his logistical support and lines of communication with the Hellespont. Second, the Persians hoped to find a strong defensive position that would not only compel Alexander to attack but also minimize his more than 2-to-1 advantage in the infantry, while capitalizing on their 2-to-1 advantage in cavalry.

In keeping with their plan, the Persians advanced from Zelea to the nearby Granicus River (today called the Kocabas Cay). The 60- to 90-foot-wide river, with its varying depth, strong current and steep, irregular bank, would pose a significant obstacle to Alexander's cavalry and would make it difficult for his phalanxes to hold formation. The Persians established a strong defensive position on the eastern bank and placed all their cavalry in the front line, creating as wide a front as possible– approximately 7,500 feet, or 1.4 miles. There, they confidently awaited the Macedonian army's arrival.

Diodorus is the only ancient author who provides even a partial Persian order of battle: Memnon of Rhodes, with a cavalry unit of unknown size and nationality, held the extreme left of the Persian forward line. To his right was Arsamenes, also with a cavalry of unknown size and nationality; then Artistes, with Paphlagonian cavalry of unknown size; and Spithridates, with Hyrcanian cavalry of unknown size. The extreme right of the Persian forward line was held by 1,000 Median cavalries and 2,000 cavalries of unknown nationality, both under the command of Rheomithres and by 2,000 Bactrian cavalry. The center was held by cavalry units of unknown size and nationality, probably under the joint command of Mithridates and Rhoesaces, and no doubt others not mentioned in ancient texts. Greek mercenaries, under

Omares, made up the mass of the infantry and were placed at the rear of the cavalry on higher ground.

Some military historians have interpreted the Persian battle array as a tactical blunder. They argue that, by placing the cavalry so close to the steep riverbank, the Persians deprived it of the opportunity to charge; and the infantry, in the rear of the cavalry, became mere observers of a struggle in which they could offer little assistance. One of the greatest of Alexander's modern biographers, Sir William Tarn, disagreed, however, stating that 'the Persian leaders had, in fact, a very gallant plan; they meant if possible to strangle the war at birth by killing Alexander.'

In ancient times, the commander's personal leadership and presence in the forefront of the battle were so important that his sudden loss, especially at the beginning of the combat, would have a demoralizing effect, possibly causing his army to panic and flee soon after his death. Thus, it seems likely that, by placing their cavalrymen in the front, the Persian leaders intended to meet Alexander's cavalry charge with their numerically– and, they believed, qualitatively–superior cavalry and simply overwhelm his horsemen.

While the Macedonian army was completing its crossing into Asia Minor, Alexander, accompanied by a portion of his royal guards, sailed ahead, steering south to visit the ruins of the nearby ancient city of Troy. There, he ceremoniously made sacrifices to the gods in honor of the legendary Greek heroes who had fallen nearly 1,000 years earlier in the Trojan War–Greece's first known invasion of Asia.

Upon rejoining his main army, Alexander received intelligence that the Persian forces were some 50 miles to the northeast. He realized that his first objective could no longer be to move south to liberate the Greek cities under Persian control since that would leave a substantial enemy force in his rear. Instead, he marched northeastward along the shore of the Hellespont and the Propontis (the present-day Sea of Marmara) with just more than 18,000 of his finest troops (13,000 infantry and 5,100 cavalries), ready to challenge the Persians to a pitched battle.

In midafternoon on the third day of marching, Alexander was not far from the Granicus when his scouts reported that the Persian army was drawn up on the east bank of the river. As the Macedonian army marched toward the river through open country, Alexander placed his heavy infantry in the center in two tandem columns, heavy cavalry on each flank and the baggage train in the rear; he then advanced in semi deployment behind a heavy screen of light cavalry and infantry.

When Macedonian General Parmenion, Alexander's second-in-command, could see the enemy's line, he studied their forces on the far bank, as well as the topography, and advised caution. He disagreed with Alexander about the battle plan, pointing out the difficulties in the river crossing and warning that an immediate attack invited disaster. Alexander, however, rejected Parmenion's advice, perhaps wanting to capitalize on the Persians' error in tactical deployment, and decided to deploy his army to attack at once.

In the center of his line, Alexander placed his six Foot Companion battalions of heavy infantry (historically referred to as phalanxes), arranged in the following order from left to right: Meleager's phalanx with 1,500 infantrymen; the phalanx of Philip, son of Amyntas, with 1,500 infantrymen; the phalanx of Amyntas, son of Andromenes, with 1,500 infantrymen; Craterus' phalanx, with 1,500 infantrymen; the phalanx of Coenus, son of

Polemocrates, with 1,500 infantrymen; and the phalanx of Perdiccas, son of Orontes, with 1,500 infantrymen. On the left of the phalanxes stood 150 Thracian Odrysian light cavalries under Agathon and 600 Greek allied heavy cavalries under Philip, son of Menelaus. On the extreme left of Alexander's line were 1,800 Thessalian heavy cavalries under Calas, joined by Parmenion, who probably stationed himself at the head of the Pharsalia squadron. On the right of the phalanxes stood, in succession: 3,000 shield bearers divided into three phalanxes of 1,000 heavy infantrymen each, all under Nicanor, son of Parmenion; a combined light mounted force of 600 Prodromoi cavalry and 150 Paeonian cavalry, commanded by Amyntas, son of Arrhabaeus; one squadron of 200 Companion heavy cavalry under Socrates, whose turn it was to take the lead that day; 1,600 Companion heavy cavalry (with Alexander stationed at the head of the royal squadron), under Philotas, son of Parmenion; 500 Agrianian light-javelin men, under Attalus; and, finally, 500 Cretan light archers, under Clearchus.

For the purpose of the command, the army was divided into two wings. The right, commanded by Alexander, consisted of the three right Foot Companion phalanxes and everything to their right; while Parmenion commanded the three left Foot Companion phalanxes and everything to their left.

As the Battle of the Granicus began, the Persian leaders, in keeping with their plan to kill Alexander, focused on the Macedonian commander in chief's movements. The glitter of his magnificent armor, the white plumes on the helmet and his entourage made him a conspicuous target. When the Persians observed Alexander at the head of the Companion cavalry on the right flank, they concluded that his intention was to attack their left. As a result, the Persians transferred some of their cavalry regiments from their center and left-center and massed them on and above the riverbank opposite Alexander to meet what they expected would be his main assault.

Once the final Persian and Macedonian battle arrays were complete, the two armies paused a moment and faced each other in silence. Then Alexander opened the battle by sending forward an advance force under the command of Amyntas. Three contingents of cavalry–the combined Prodromoi and Paeonian force, along with Socrates' Companion squadron–totaling 950 horsemen, and one phalanx of infantry (1,000 soldiers) made a feint attack on the Persians' extreme left flank, with Socrates' squadron leading the way.

Arrian, a 2nd-century Greek historian whose account of the battle is the most comprehensive and reliable, described the hard-fought cavalry action that ensued in the river and on its bank: 'At the point where the vanguard under Amyntas and Socrates touched the bank, the Persians shot volleys on them from above, some hurling their javelins into the river from their commanding position on the bank, others going down to the stream on the more level ground. There was a great shoving by the cavalry, as some were trying to get out of the river, others to stop them, great showers of Persian javelins, much thrusting of Macedonian spears. But the Macedonians, much outnumbered, came off badly in the first onslaught; they were defending themselves from the river on ground that was not firm and was beneath the enemy's while the Persians had the advantage of the bank; in particular, the flower of the Persian cavalry was posted here, and Memnon's sons and Memnon himself ventured their lives with them. The first Macedonians who came to grips with the Persians were cut down, despite their valor.'

Although the relatively weak Macedonian advance force met with predictably intense resistance and suffered heavy losses, it succeeded in drawing the Persian left-flank cavalry out of their formations. Once that was achieved, Alexander, with trumpets blaring his commands, launched his main assault, leading his famous Companion cavalry, the elite of the army, forward toward the now-disorganized Persian cavalry. With Alexander at the head of the royal squadron, the six other Companion cavalry squadrons crossed the river and fought their way up to its eastern bank, as the Persians hurled their javelins down upon them.

Arrian described the fighting at that point: 'Though the fighting was on horseback, it was more like an infantry battle, horse entangled with horse, man with man in the struggle, the Macedonians trying to push the Persians once and for all from the bank and force them on to the level ground, the Persians trying to bar their landing and thrust them back again into the river.' Meanwhile, the remainder of Alexander's right-wing–the Agrianian javelin men, Cretan archers, two phalanxes of shield bearers and three right phalanxes of Foot Companions–also advanced, with trumpets and battle cries resounding as they entered the river.

When the Persian leaders recognized Alexander, they rode to engage him in a fierce hand-to-hand struggle. The battle became a series of heroic duels between individuals rather than a fight between cavalry units. During the struggle, Alexander's long Macedonian cavalry lance, or sarissa, was splintered, and he called upon Aretas, one of his Companions, to provide him with another. Aretas' own weapon had suffered the same misfortune, so Alexander continued fighting bravely with the aft point (Sauter). He had no sooner received another sarissa from the Companion Demaratus than the Persian cavalry commander Mithridates appeared at the head of a squadron. Alexander rode forward and struck the Persian leader in the face with his sarissa, killing him instantly.

Rhoades, another Persian nobleman, rode up and with his scimitar sliced off part of Alexander's helmet, causing a minor wound. Then Alexander drove his sarissa through Rhoesaces' breastplate and into his chest, bringing him to the ground. A third Persian leader, Spithridates, was close behind Alexander and raised his scimitar to strike, but Cleitus, commander of the royal squadron to whom the king's safety was entrusted, anticipated the blow and severed the Persian's sword arm, saving Alexander's life. Although the Persians maintained a vigorous resistance throughout the bitter struggle, they failed to withstand the charge of the Companion cavalry and were continually pushed back. Arrian wrote, 'The Persians were now being roughly handled from all quarters; they and their horses were struck in the face with lances [sarissas], they were being pushed back by the [Companion] cavalry, and were suffering heavily from the light troops, who had intermingled with the cavalry.' With the Companion cavalry's fierce onslaught opening the way, the remainder of Alexander's right-wing crossed the Granicus. They slowly but steadily drove the Persians farther back, gaining the level ground above the steep riverbank.

Meanwhile, Parmenion's left-wing had also advanced and secured a footing. According to Diodorus, the Thessalian cavalry 'won a great reputation for valor because of the skillful handling of their squadrons and their unmatched fighting quality.' Although there are no details about the role of Parmenion's left-wing in the battle, its advance

47

was probably delayed until Alexander's attack was well underway. At the later great battles of Issus and Gaugamela, the Macedonians used a strong defensive left wing at the onset of the battle to balance and safeguard their bold offensive operations on the right.

As a result of the loss of so many of its leaders, the opposition offered by the Persian cavalry deteriorated rapidly. The Persian line first began to give way at the point where Alexander was engaged; then the whole center collapsed. Once the center had caved in, both wings of the Persian cavalry–Memnon among them–panicked and fled. The Macedonians could not pursue the fleeing cavalry very far, however. The Persian Greek mercenary infantry, who up to that point had taken no part in the battle, still held their ground and stood in Alexander's path. The mercenary contingent (perhaps 3,000 troops) presented Alexander with terms under which it would surrender, but he rejected them and ordered his phalanxes to attack the mercenaries in the front, while his cavalry assaulted them on their unprotected flanks and rear. With the exception of 2,000 prisoners–and possibly a few others who threw themselves on the ground and concealed themselves among the dead–the mercenaries were cut down.

The ancient historians' accounts vary widely as to the losses on both sides. In view of the swiftness of the battle, Arrian probably provided the most credible statistics, although the Macedonian figures are suspiciously low and the Persian numbers perhaps slightly elevated. According to him, Macedonian losses totaled 115 killed–85 cavalry (including 25 Companions from Socrates' squadron, who fell in the advance force) and 30 infantry. No doubt the number of wounded was considerably higher. Persian losses amounted to 4,000 killed–about

1,000 cavalry and perhaps 3,000 Greek mercenaries–along with with 2,000 taken prisoner.

Among the Persian high command known to have died in the attempt to slay Alexander were: Spithridates, satrap of Ionia and Lydia; Mithrobuzanes, satrap of Cappadocia; Mithridates, son-in-law of King Darius; Arbupales, grandson of King Artaxerxes II; Phranaces, brother-in-law of King Darius; Rhoesaces, brother of Spithridates; Omares, commander of the Greek mercenaries; Niphates, perhaps a cavalry commander; Petines, perhaps a cavalry commander; and Artistes, satrap of Hellespontine Phrygia (the province in which the battle took place), who fled and later committed suicide, according to Arrian, 'because the blame of the present blunder seemed to the Persians to lie at his door.'

By Alexander's order, all who had fallen in the Battle of the Granicus, including the Persian leaders and Greek mercenaries, were buried with military honors. To the surviving relatives of his fallen soldiers, Alexander granted immunity from taxation and public service. He ordered Lysippus, considered perhaps the greatest sculptor of the day, to make bronze statues of the 25 Companion cavalrymen who fell in the initial feint attack. The statues were eventually set up in Darum, a city in Macedon at the foot of Mount Olympus. Alexander visited his wounded, examined their injuries and, according to Arrian, gave every soldier an opportunity to recount–and perhaps exaggerate–his deeds.

The Persian commanders had not kept pace with military developments in Greece, including the tactics and quality of the Macedonian army, in the two decades prior to Alexander's invasion. Believing themselves to be a match for Alexander in the field, the Persians, who failed to use their professional infantry, simply counted on their numerically superior cavalry and their personal bravery to secure a victory. The resulting lack of coordination between horse and foot violated a principle of integrated armies that even the Persians had long understood.

According to historian E.W. Davis, however, the Persians' greatest weakness was that the 'Persian army seems to have been commanded by a committee [and] it may be that we do not have a Persian battle-plan at all, only a blotched compromise between several rival plans.' The Persian defeat, resulting in the loss of so many satraps and others in the Persian high command, was so overwhelming that no other army could be reassembled to challenge Alexander in all of Asia Minor.

On the other hand, the Battle of the Granicus highlighted Alexander's remarkable insights into the development of the battle, his anticipation of the enemy's reactions, his sense of timing, and especially his coordination of heavy infantry, heavy cavalry, light cavalry and light infantry in a single attack. Alexander calculated that, although his cavalry was outnumbered 2-to-1, it was superior in skill and discipline. His cavalrymen were shock troops, armed with long sarissas, and were more accustomed to strong hand-to-hand fighting than were the Persian cavalrymen. The latter were armed with short javelins (designed more for throwing than for thrusting) and scimitars, both of which were ineffective against the Macedonian sarissas.

Alexander also realized that his attacking cavalry had a great advantage over its Persian counterpart, whose defensive role forfeited its mobility and whose faulty deployment negated its advantage in numbers. Alexander's light infantry archers and javelin men, interspersed among his Companion cavalry, also inflicted much damage and further helped to offset the Persian cavalry's numerical superiority.

Alexander's heroic leadership, as he fought in the thick of battle and narrowly escaped death, earned him what Diodorus called the 'palm for bravery' and gave him his first great victory over the Persians, opening the way to western and southern Asia Minor. From the spoils of that success, Alexander sent 300 suits of Persian armor to the Parthenon in Athens, to remind the Greeks that this victory was part of the war of revenge against the Persians and to stir Greek enthusiasm. With the triumph at the Granicus, the Greek cities of Asia Minor were liberated from Persian rule–and the beachhead was established for later campaigns deeper in Persian territory.

CHAPTER 5

Indian Campaign

Alexander invaded India expecting a heroic entry but in the end, it turned into a humiliating retreat. If you've seen the epic movie Alexander by Oliver Stone, you wouldn't have missed the noted American director's commentary at the end where he talks about the battle of Multan. Stone – with smugness more suited to a conqueror than a director – narrates how the Macedonian king single-handedly jumped into combat against 1000 Indian defenders, inspiring his dithering Greek soldiers and commanders to storm their fort.

To the victors go the spoils, so if the Greeks and Macedonians were really victorious, as European accounts narrate, then why did they leave India so soon? After all, over 99 percent of the country was still unconquered. And why did the retreating army resemble a defeated brood – rather than a triumphant force – trekking across inhospitable areas, losing an estimated 60,000 men in the process?

The fact is that Alexander's Indian campaign was a complete disaster for the Greeks. They were traumatized after the first few battles, losing most of their men in ferocious battles against Indian warriors, the likes of whom they had never encountered before.

Let's flashback to history! In 326 BC the formidable Greek-Macedonian army entered India. It was the first time Europeans and Indians first looked into one another's faces; the first meeting of the two halves of the Aryan people since their forefathers had parted centuries before.

In his first encounter, Alexander fought for four days against the warlike people of the city of Massaga in Swat valley. On the first day of this battle, Alexander was injured and forced to retreat. The same fate awaited him on the second and third days. When Alexander lost men and was on the verge of defeat, he called for a truce. Clearly, the Indians weren't aware of the Trojan horse episode, for the Greeks slaughtered the unaware and unarmed citizens of Massaga as they slept in the night of the fourth day believing that the battle was over.

In the second and third battles at Bazira and Ora, Alexander faced a similar fate and again resorted to treachery to defeat those fortresses. But the fierce resistance put up by the Indian defenders had reduced the strength – and perhaps the will – of the until then all-conquering Macedonian-led army.

Greek histories record that Alexander's hardest battle was the Battle of Hydaspes (Jhelum) in which he faced King Puru, the Yaduvanshi king of the Paurava kingdom of Punjab. Paurava was a prosperous Indian kingdom on the banks of the river Jhelum, and Puru – described in Greek accounts as Porus and standing over seven feet tall – was a generous monarch.

Perhaps, he was generous to a fault. Legend has it that ahead of Alexander's entry into India, his Persian wife Roxana, the daughter of the defeated Persian king Darius, arrived in Paurava to meet King Puru, who was preparing for war against the foreign invader.

Roxana gained access to Puru, and through the bond of rakhi, declared herself his sister. She then begged Puru to spare her husband's life if he encountered the

Macedonian king in battle. The large-hearted Indian king agreed to this bizarre request.

In the autumn of 326BC, the Greek and Paurava armies faced each other across the banks of the river Jhelum in Punjab. By all accounts, it was an awe-inspiring spectacle. The Greeks had 34,000 infantry and 7000 cavalries. This number was boosted further by their Persian allies.

Facing this tumultuous force led by the genius of Alexander was the Paurava army of 20,000 infantry, 2000 cavalry, and 200 war elephants. Being a comparatively small kingdom by Indian standards, Paurava couldn't have had such a large standing army, so it's likely many of its defenders were hastily armed civilians.

According to Greek sources, for several days the armies eyeballed each other across the river. They write Alexander could not move his army across the river because it was swollen from the rains.

A lame excuse is not found in history! Alexander's army had crossed the Hellespont, a 1-8 km wide strip of sea that divides Asia and Europe, and which was well defended by the Persians. In comparison, crossing the narrower Jhelum against a much smaller adversary should have been a far easier task.

In reality, the Greek-Macedonian force, after having lost several thousand soldiers fighting much smaller Indian mountain cities, were terrified at the prospect of fighting the fierce Paurava army. They had also heard about the havoc that Indian war elephants were supposed to create among enemy ranks. The modern equivalent of battle tanks, the war elephants also scared the wits out of the horses in the Greek cavalry.

In the Battle of Hydaspes, the Indians fought with bravery and war skills that no other army had shown against the Greeks. In the first charge by the Indians, Puru's brother Amar killed Alexander's favorite horse Bucephalus, forcing Alexander to dismount. In battles outside India, the elite Macedonian bodyguards had not allowed a single enemy soldier to deliver so much as a scratch on their king's body, let alone slay his mount. Yet in this battle with the Paurava army, not only was Alexander injured, the Indians killed Nicaea, one of the leading Greek commanders.

According to the Roman historian Marcus Justinus, the battle was savagely fought. Puru challenged Alexander, who charged him on horseback. In the ensuing duel, Alexander fell off his horse and was at the mercy of the Indian king's spear (and this is where legend meets history) when Puru perhaps remembered his promise to his rakhi sister (probably a Trojan horse sent in by the Greeks). He spared the Macedonian's life, and Alexander's bodyguards quickly carried off their king.

The Greeks may claim victory but if Alexander's troops were so badly mauled by the petty regional fiefdoms, how could they have crushed the comparatively stronger army of Puru? An unbiased re-examination of contemporary histories suggests the Greeks probably lost the battle and Alexander sued for peace.

In his epic volume, The Life and Exploits of Alexander, a series of translations of the Ethiopic histories of Alexander, E.A.W. Budge, Egyptologist, orientalist, and philologist, has given a vivid account of the Macedonian's misadventure in India.

According to Budge, who worked for the British Museum in the early part of the 20th century, in the Battle of Hydaspes, the Indians destroyed the majority of Alexander's cavalry? Realizing that if he were to continue fighting he would be completely ruined, the Macedonian requested Puru to stop fighting. True to Indian traditions, the magnanimous Indian king spared the life of the surrendered enemy. A peace treaty was signed, and

Alexander helped Puru in annexing other territories to his kingdom.

The Greek geographer Strabo complains in the Geographika that all who wrote about Alexander preferred the marvelous to the true. Certainly, he alludes to Alexander's original propaganda to glorify his struggle in the East. He created his own mystified version of the campaign, transforming it into a search for divine traces. For instance, the ancient Greeks believed that Dionysius, one of their chief Gods, had his origins in India. They also lamented that the legendary Heracles had failed in his Indian campaigns. Alexander wanted to succeed in the Dionysius' homeland where the great Heracles himself had failed. Also, while the ostensible purpose of Alexander's campaign was to avenge the Persians' destruction of Athens, the real reason was that he had many enemy's among Macedonia's elite, and a state of continuous war kept the warriors and public busy. Indeed, he simply could not afford to go back defeated. The web of lies he and his entourage spun was in keeping with that scheme.

Plutarch, the Greek historian, and biographer, says of the Battle of Hydaspes: "The combat with Porus took the edge off the Macedonians' courage, and stayed their further progress into India. For having found it hard enough to defeat an enemy who brought but 20,000 foot and 2000 horse into the field, they thought they had reason to oppose Alexander's design of leading them on to pass the Ganges, on the further side of which was covered with multitudes of enemies."

Indeed, on the other side of the Ganges was the mighty kingdom of Magadh, ruled by the ferocious and wily Nandas, who commanded one of the largest standing armies in the world. According to Plutarch, the courage of the Greeks evaporated when they came to know that the

Nandas "were awaiting them with 200,000 infantry, 80,000 cavalries, 8000 war chariots, and 6000 fighting elephants". Undoubtedly, the Greeks would have walked into a slaughterhouse.

Still 400 km from the Ganges, the Indian heartland, Alexander ordered a retreat to great jubilation among his soldiers. The celebrations were premature. On its way south towards the mouth of the Indus river, Alexander's army was constantly harried by Indian soldiers. When the Greeks pillaged villages, the Indians retaliated. In some kingdoms, the Indian soldiers simply fell upon the Greeks because they wouldn't tolerate foreigners invading their country.

In a campaign at Sangala in Punjab, the Indian attack was so ferocious that it completely destroyed the Greek cavalry, forcing Alexander the great to attack foot. However, in the following counterattack, Alexander took the fort and sold the surviving Indians into slavery. (That's another facet of the Macedonian that is glossed over by western historians; Alexander was far from being a noble king, and on the contrary, was a vicious and cruel person.)

His battle with the Malavs of Multan – the most warlike people of Punjab – is perhaps the most recounted. In the hotly contested battle, Alexander was felled by a Malav warrior whose arrow pierced the Macedonian's breastplate and lodged in his ribs. The Indian warrior seeing the enemy king fall advanced to take his armor but was checked by Alexander's bodyguards who rushed into the battle to save their king. The Macedonians later stormed the fort and in revenge killed every one of the 17,000 inhabitants of the fort, including women and children. Alexander never recovered from the wound and died in Babylon (Iraq) at the age of 33.

Western historians depict the Battle of Hydaspes as a clash of the organized West and the muddling East. That one battle is portrayed as the Greek conquest of India, while the fact is that Alexander merely probed the north-western extremity of India. Puru was by any reckoning a minor king and doesn't even merit a mention in Indian accounts.

The Greek invasion of India was a popular subject in Greece and Rome for many centuries. The Alexander romance even entered medieval European literature and religion. Much later it became the fountainhead of inspiration for the colonization of the east, especially India. Yet within a few years after Alexander's retreat, the Indians drove the Greeks out of India. Inspired by the master strategist Chanakya, Chandragupta Maurya, the founder of the Mauryan dynasty, defeated Seleucus Necator, Alexander's satrap. This was quite unlike the rest of Alexander's other territorial conquests. It took the Sassanians 500 years to get back Persia from the Greeks. The Parthians were able to depose the Greeks 250 years after Alexander. Egypt never recovered its lost glory.

Arrian, the Roman biographer of Alexander, says the only 'victory' celebration by Alexander's troops was after the battle with Puru. Surprising – that Alexander's troops did not celebrate any victory, till the very end of the campaign. Was it, instead, a celebration that they had escaped with their lives?

The Greek retreat from India shows clear signs of a defeated force. Indeed, if the Greek and Macedonian soldiers were really that tired of fighting, as western historians claim, then the 'triumphant' troops should have returned via the same route they arrived. But instead, they preferred to trek south through unknown and hostile lands in Punjab, Sindh, and Balochistan. The only explanation is that they didn't want to face the mountain kingdoms again.

Also, it's a myth that the Greeks and Macedonians were tired of fighting and were hankering to meet their families. Alexander's army had a system of rotation where large batches of soldiers were released to return home (with sufficient gold, slaves and other spoils of war) after major victories. In their place, fresh troops eager to do battle (and lured by the promise of more loot) were constantly trickling in from Greece.

There is more indirect evidence of the lack of major Greek victories in India. The booty that fell into Greek hands after they defeated the Persians in the Battle of Gaugamela in 331 BC is estimated at 100,000 talents (more than 2,500,000 kilos) of gold. However, there is no mention of any large booty captured from India – strange because those days India was pretty much swimming in gold and other precious metals and stones. So it can be safely argued that Alexander failed to get his hands on a substantial booty because he never won any substantial victories.

On the contrary, Alexander gave King Ambhi, the ruler of Taxila, 1000 talents (over 25,000 kilos) of gold to fight alongside him in the battle against Puru. That's even stranger! Because Greek sources say Ambhi voluntarily came over to their side. So why a willing ally was paid such a large amount? If Alexander was really rolling through India, it's inconceivable he would pay off a minor king to ally with him.

Almost all accounts of Alexander's campaigns in India have been based on modern European translations of ancient texts. Unless Indian universities and think tanks look at the original Greek, Roman, Ethiopian and Egyptian manuscripts, a clear picture will not emerge. European translations are mostly slanted for obvious reasons. The Greek and Roman civilizations are the wellspring of western thought, science, culture, religion, and philosophy; a defeat for Alexander 'the Great', would be a blow for all that he represents – especially the triumph of the West over the East.

CHAPTER 6

Last Years in Persia

Alexander had set his mind on the Persian expedition. He had grown up to the idea. Moreover, he needed the wealth of Persia if he was to maintain the army built by Philip and pay off the 500 talents he owed. The exploits of the Ten Thousand, Greek soldiers of fortune, and of Agesilaus of Sparta, in successfully campaigning in Persian territory had revealed the vulnerability of the Persian Empire. With a good cavalry force, Alexander could expect to defeat any Persian army. In spring 334 he crossed the Dardanelles, leaving Antipater, who had already faithfully served his father, as his deputy in Europe with over 13,000 men; he himself commanded about 30,000 foot and over 5,000 cavalries, of whom nearly 14,000 were Macedonians and about 7,000 allies sent by the Greek League. This army was to prove remarkable for its balanced combination of arms. Much work fell on the light-armed Cretan and Macedonian archers, Thracians, and the Agrianian javelin men. But in a pitched battle, the striking force was the cavalry, and the core of the army, should the issue still remain undecided after the cavalry charge, was the infantry phalanx, 9,000 strong, armed with 13-foot spears and shields, and the 3,000 men of the royal battalions, the hypaspists. Alexander's second in command was Parmenio, who had secured a foothold in Asia Minor during Philip's lifetime; many of his family and supporters were entrenched in positions of responsibility. The army was accompanied by surveyors, engineers, architects, scientists, court officials, and historians; from the outset, Alexander seems to have envisaged an unlimited operation.

After visiting Ilium (Troy), a romantic gesture inspired by Homer, he confronted his first Persian army, led by three satraps, at the Granicus (modern Kocabas) River, near the Sea of Marmara (May/June 334). The Persian plan to tempt Alexander across the river and kill him in the melee almost succeeded, but the Persian line broke, and Alexander's victory was complete. Darius's Greek mercenaries were largely massacred, but 2,000 survivors were sent back to Macedonia in chains. This victory exposed western Asia Minor to the Macedonians, and most cities hastened to open their gates. The tyrants were expelled and (in contrast to Macedonian policy in Greece) democracies were installed. Alexander thus underlined his Panhellenic policy, already symbolized in the sending of 300 panoplies (sets of armor) taken at the Granicus as an offering dedicated to Athena at Athens by "Alexander son of Philip and the Greeks (except the Spartans) from the barbarians who inhabit Asia." (This formula, cited by the Greek historian Arrian in his history of Alexander's campaigns, is noteworthy for its omission of any reference to Macedonia.) But the cities remained de facto under Alexander, and his appointment of Calas as satrap of Hellespontine Phrygia reflected his claim to succeed the Great King of Persia. When Miletus, encouraged by the proximity of the Persian fleet, resisted, Alexander took it by assault, but, refusing a naval battle, he disbanded his own costly navy and announced that he would "defeat the Persian fleet on land," by occupying the coastal cities. In Caria, Halicarnassus resisted and was stormed, but Ada, the widow, and sister of the satrap Idrieus adopted Alexander as her son and, after expelling her brother Pixodarus, Alexander restored her to her satrapy. Some parts of Caria held out, however, until 332. In winter 334–333 Alexander conquered western Asia Minor, subduing the hill tribes of Lycia and Pisidia, and in spring 333 he advanced along the coastal road to Perga, passing the cliffs of Mount Climax, thanks to a fortunate change of wind. The fall in the level of the sea was interpreted as a mark of divine favor by Alexander's flatterers, including the historian Callisthenes. At Gordium in Phrygia, tradition records his cutting of the Gordian knot, which could only be loosed by the man who was to rule Asia; but this story may be apocryphal or at least distorted. At this point, Alexander benefitted from the sudden death of Memnon, the competent Greek commander of the Persian fleet. From Gordium he pushed on to Ancyra (modern Ankara) and thence south through Cappadocia and the Cilician Gates (modern Külek Bogazi); a fever held him up for a time in Cilicia. Meanwhile, Darius with his Grand Army had advanced northward on the eastern side of Mount Amanus. Intelligence on both sides was faulty, and Alexander was already encamped by Myriandrus (near modern Iskenderun, Turkey) when he learned that Darius was astride his line of communications at Issus, north of Alexander's position (autumn 333). Turning, Alexander found Darius drawn up along the Pinarus River. In the battle that followed, Alexander won a decisive victory. The struggle turned into a Persian rout and Darius fled, leaving his family in Alexander's hands; the women were treated with chivalrous care.

From Issus Alexander marched south into Syria and Phoenicia, his object being to isolate the Persian fleet from its bases and so to destroy it as an effective fighting force. The Phoenician cities Marathus and Aradus came over quietly, and Parmenio was sent ahead to secure

Damascus and its rich booty, including Darius's war chest. In reply to a letter from Darius offering peace, Alexander replied arrogantly, recapitulating the historic wrongs of Greece and demanding unconditional surrender to himself as lord of Asia. After taking Byblos (modern Jubayl) and Sidon (Arabic? ayda), he met with a check at Tyre, where he was refused entry into the island city. He thereupon prepared to use all methods of siegecraft to take it, but the Tyrians resisted, holding out for seven months. In the meantime (winter 333–332) the Persians had counterattacked by land in Asia Minor—where they were defeated by Antigonus, the satrap of Greater Phrygia—and by sea, recapturing a number of cities and islands.

While the siege of Tyre was in progress, Darius sent a new offer: he would pay a huge ransom of 10,000 talents for his family and cede all his lands west of the Euphrates. "I would accept," Parmenio is reported to have said, "were I Alexander"; "I too," was the famous retort, "were I Parmenio." The storming of Tyre in July 332 was Alexander's greatest military achievement; it was attended with great carnage and the sale of the women and children into slavery. Leaving Parmenio in Syria, Alexander advanced south without opposition until he reached Gaza on its high mound; their bitter resistance halted him for two months, and he sustained a serious shoulder wound during a sortie. There is no basis for the tradition that he turned aside to visit Jerusalem.

In November 332 he reached Egypt. The people welcomed him as their deliverer, and the Persian satrap Mazaces wisely surrendered. At Memphis Alexander sacrificed to Apis, the Greek term for Hapi, the sacred Egyptian bull, and was crowned with the traditional double crown of the pharaohs; the native priests were placated and their religion encouraged. He spent the winter organizing Egypt, where he employed Egyptian governors, keeping the army under a separate Macedonian command. He founded the city of Alexandria near the western arm of the Nile on a fine site between the sea and Lake Mareotis, protected by the island of Pharos, and had it laid out by the Rhodian architect Deinocrates. He is also said to have sent an expedition to discover the causes of the flooding of the Nile. From Alexandria he marched along the coast to Paraetonium and from there inland to visit the celebrated oracle of the god Amon (at Siwah); the difficult journey was later embroidered with flattering legends. On his reaching the oracle in its oasis, the priest gave him the traditional salutation of a pharaoh, as a son of Amon; Alexander consulted the god on the success of his expedition but revealed the reply to no one. Later the incident was to contribute to the story that he was the son of Zeus and, thus, to his "deification." In spring 331 he returned to Tyre, appointed a Macedonian satrap for Syria, and prepared to advance into Mesopotamia. His conquest of Egypt had completed his control of the whole eastern Mediterranean coast.

In July 331 Alexander was at Thapsacus on the Euphrates. Instead of taking the direct route down the river to Babylon, he made across northern Mesopotamia toward the Tigris, and Darius, learning of this move from an advance force sent under Mazaeus to the Euphrates crossing, marched up the Tigris to oppose him. The decisive battle of the war was fought on October 31, on the plain of Gaugamela between Nineveh and Arbela. Alexander pursued the defeated Persian forces for 35 miles to Arbela, but Darius escaped with his Bactrian cavalry and Greek mercenaries into Media.

Alexander now occupied Babylon, city, and province; Mazaeus, who surrendered it, was confirmed as satrap in conjunction with a Macedonian troop commander, and quite exceptionally was granted the right to coin. As in Egypt, the local priesthood was encouraged. Susa, the capital, also surrendered, releasing huge treasures amounting to 50,000 gold talents; here Alexander established Darius's family in comfort. Crushing the mountain tribe of the Ouxians, he now pressed on over the Zagros range into Persia proper and, successfully turning the Pass of the Persian Gates, held by the satrap Ariobarzanes, he entered Persepolis and Pasargadae. At Persepolis he ceremonially burned down the palace of Xerxes, as a symbol that the Panhellenic war of revenge was at an end; for such seems the probable significance of an act that tradition later explained as a drunken frolic inspired by Thaïs, an Athenian courtesan. In spring 330 Alexander marched north into Media and occupied its capital. The Thessalians and Greek allies were sent home; henceforward he was waging a purely personal war. As Mazaeus's appointment indicated, Alexander's views on the empire were changing. He had come to envisage a joint ruling people consisting of Macedonians and Persians, and this served to augment the misunderstanding that now arose between him and his people. Before continuing his pursuit of Darius, who had retreated into Bactria, he assembled all the Persian treasure and entrusted it to Harpalus, who was to hold it at Ecbatana as chief treasurer. Parmenio was also left behind in Media to control communications; the presence of this older man had perhaps become irksome.

In midsummer 330 Alexander set out for the eastern provinces at a high speed via Rhagae (modern Rayy, near Tehran) and the Caspian Gates, where he learned that Bessus, the satrap of Bactria, had deposed Darius. After a skirmish near modern Shahrud, the usurper had Darius stabbed and left him to die. Alexander sent his body for burial with due honors in the royal tombs at Persepolis.

Campaign eastward to Central Asia
Darius's death left no obstacle to Alexander's claim to be Great King, and a Rhodian inscription of this year (330) calls him "lord of Asia"—i.e., of the Persian empire; soon afterward his Asian coins carry the title of king. Crossing the Elburz Mountains to the Caspian, he seized Zadracarta in Hyrcania and received the submission of a group of satrap's and Persian notables, some of whom he confirmed in their offices; in a diversion westward, perhaps to modern Amol, he reduced the Mardi, a mountain people who inhabited the Elburz Mountains. He also accepted the surrender of Darius's Greek mercenaries. His advance eastward was now rapid. In Aria, he reduced Satibarzanes, who had offered submission only to revolt, and he founded Alexandria of the Arians (modern Herat). At Phrada in Drangiana (either near modern Nad-e? Ali in Seistan or farther north at Farah), he, at last, took steps to destroy Parmenio and his family. Philotas, Parmenio's son, commander of the elite Companion cavalry, was implicated in an alleged plot against Alexander's life, condemned by the army, and executed; and a secret message was sent to Cleander, Parmenio's second in command, who obediently assassinated him. This ruthless action excited widespread horror but strengthened Alexander's position relative to his critics and those whom he regarded as his father's men. All Parmenio's adherents were now eliminated and men close to Alexander promoted. The Companion cavalry was reorganized in two sections, each containing four squadrons (now known as hierarchies); one group was commanded by Alexander's oldest friend, Hephaestion, the other by

Cleitus, an older man. From Phrada, Alexander pressed on during the winter of 330–329 up the valley of the Helmand River, through Arachosia, and over the mountains past the site of modern Kabul into the country of the Paropamisadae, where he founded Alexandria by the Caucasus.

Bessus was now in Bactria raising a national revolt in the eastern satrapies with the usurped title of Great King. Crossing the Hindu Kush northward over the Khawak Pass (11,650 feet [3,550 metres]), Alexander brought his army, despite food shortages, to Drapsaca (sometimes identified with modern Banu [Andarab], probably farther north at Qunduz); outflanked, Bessus fled beyond the Oxus (modern Amu Darya), and Alexander, marching west to Bactra-Zariaspa (modern Balkh [Wazirabad] in Afghanistan), appointed loyal satraps in Bactria and Aria. Crossing the Oxus, he sent his general Ptolemy in pursuit of Bessus, who had meanwhile been overthrown by the Sogdian Spitamenes. Bessus was captured, flogged, and sent to Bactra, where he was later mutilated after the Persian manner (losing his nose and ears); in due course, he was publicly executed at Ecbatana.

From Maracanda (modern Samarkand) Alexander advanced by way of Cyropolis to the Jaxartes (modern Syrdarya), the boundary of the Persian empire. There he broke the opposition of the Scythian nomads by his use of catapults and, after defeating them in a battle on the north bank of the river, pursued them into the interior. On the site of modern Leninabad (Khojent) on the Jaxartes, he founded a city, Alexandria Estate, "the farthest." Meanwhile, Spitamenes had raised all Sogdiana in revolt behind him, bringing in the Massagetai, a people of the Shaka confederacy. It took Alexander until the autumn of 328 to crush the most determined opponent he encountered in his campaigns. Later in the same year, he attacked Oxyartes and the remaining barons who held out in the hills of Paraetacene (modern Tajikistan); volunteers seized the crag on which Oxyartes had his stronghold, and among the captives was his daughter, Roxana. In reconciliation, Alexander married her, and the rest of his opponents were either won over or crushed.

An incident that occurred at Maracanda widened the breach between Alexander and many of his Macedonians. He murdered Cleitus, one of his most trusted commanders, in a drunken quarrel, but his excessive display of remorse led the army to pass a decree convicting Cleitus posthumously of treason. The event marked a step in Alexander's progress toward Eastern absolutism, and this growing attitude found its outward expression in his use of Persian royal dress. Shortly afterward, at Bactra, he attempted to impose the Persian court ceremonial, involving prostration (proskynesis), on the Greeks and Macedonians too, but to them, this custom, habitual for Persians entering the king's presence, implied an act of worship and was intolerable before a human. Even Callisthenes, historian and nephew of Aristotle, whose ostentatious flattery had perhaps encouraged Alexander to see himself in the role of a god, refused to abase himself. Macedonian laughter caused the experiment to the founder, and Alexander abandoned it. Shortly afterward, however, Callisthenes was held to be privy to a conspiracy among the royal pages and was executed (or died in prison; accounts vary); resentment of this action alienated sympathy from Alexander within the Peripatetic school of philosophers, with which Callisthenes had close connections.

CHAPTER 7

Death and Succession

Alexander the Great died somewhat mysteriously at the age of 32 on the afternoon of June 10-June 11, 323 B.C.E., Alexander died of a mysterious illness in the palace of Nebuchadrezzar II of Babylon. He was only 33 years old. Various theories have been proposed for the cause of his death which include poisoning by the sons of Antipater, murder by his wife Roxana, and sickness due to a relapse of malaria he had contracted in 336 B.C.E.

The poisoning theory derives from the traditional story universally held in antiquity. Alexander, coming to Babylon, had at long last disaffected enough of his senior officers that they formed a coalition against him and murdered both him and Hephaestion within a space of only a few months, intending on ending his increasingly unpopular policies of orientalism and ending any further military adventures. The original story stated that Aristotle, who'd recently seen his nephew executed by Alexander for treason, mixed the poison, that Cassander, son of Antipater, viceroy of Greece, brought it to Alexander in Babylon in a mule's hoof, and that Alexander's royal cupbearer, a son-in-law of Antipater, administered it. All had powerful motivations for seeing Alexander gone, and all were none the worse for it after his death. However, many other scholars maintain that Alexander was not poisoned, but died of natural causes, malaria being the most popular. Various other theories have been advanced stating that the king may have died from other illnesses as well, including the West Nile virus. These theories often cite the fact that Alexander's health had fallen to dangerously low levels after years of overdrinking and suffering several appalling wounds (including one in India that nearly claimed his life), and that it was only a matter of time before one sickness or another finally killed him.

Neither story is conclusive. Alexander's death has been reinterpreted many times over the centuries, and each generation offers a new take on it. What is certain is that Alexander died of a high fever in early June of 323 B.C.E. On his death bed, his marshals asked him who he bequeathed his kingdom to—as Alexander had only one heir, it was a question of vital importance. He answered famously, "The strongest." Before dying, his final words were "I foresee a great funeral contest over me." Alexander's "funeral games," where his marshals fought it out over control of his empire, lasted for nearly 40 years.

Alexander's death has been surrounded by as much controversy as many of the events of his life. Before long, accusations of foul play were being thrown about by his generals at one another, making it incredibly hard for a modern historian to sort out the propaganda and the half-truths from the actual events. No contemporary source can be fully trusted because of the incredible level of self-serving recording, and as a result, what truly happened to Alexander the Great may never be known.

According to legend, Alexander was preserved in a clay vessel full of honey (which acts as a preservative) and interred in a glass coffin. According to Aelian (Varia Historia 12.64), Ptolemy I of Egypt stole the body and brought it to Alexandria, where it was on display until Late Antiquity. Its current whereabouts are unknown.

The so-called "Alexander Sarcophagus," discovered near Sidon and now in the Istanbul Archaeological Museum, is now generally thought to be that of Abdylonymus, whom Hephaestion appointed as the king of Sidon by Alexander's order. The sarcophagus depicts Alexander and his companions hunting and in battle with the Persians and after this, the great army would never be the same.

Legacy

Alexander the Great is one of the most famous figures from Greek history, even though many ancient Greeks would not have considered him a "real Greek." This four-week series led by Associate Professor History Angela Ziskowski will explore the ascent of the Macedonian state through the succession and legacy of Alexander the Great. The series begins with an exploration of the meteoric rise of the kingdom of Macedon under the leadership of Alexander's father, Philip II—who created an ideal situation for his son to take control of much of the ancient Mediterranean world and beyond. In week two, we will examine how Alexander took control of the Macedonian kingdom after the death of his father and went on to carry out one of the largest military campaigns in history, conquering territory from Greece to India. Week three explores how Alexander's success and fame can be attributed to his personality and his control of the depiction of his image in visual culture. The last session looks at Alexander's Hellenistic successors and the ways in which much of the Mediterranean and even parts of Asia continued to be controlled by the Greco-Macedonians for hundreds of years to come, a major part of Alexander's lasting impact on western and eastern history.

The marriage to a much younger woman, and a Macedonian one at that seems to have been the final straw in a disintegrating relationship between Olympias and Philip. She fled into exile, briefly taking Alexander with her, and plotted revenge. Whether she and Alexander had anything to do with it or not- historians disagree- Philip was assassinated and, after a brief tussle, Alexander assumed the throne as king of Macedon. He was twenty. The enemies of Philip rejoiced, chortling that they now only had a boy to contend with.

Alexander was not a neophyte, either as a ruler or military commander and he had the benefit of experienced and loyal generals. The legacy handed down from Philip included these and a powerful and united Macedon. Without that, historians agree, the achievements of Alexander would have been impossible. He was as well-equipped for the task as one could have expected, given his young age. His father had provided him with the best possible schooling, engaging a number of tutors, including Aristotle, to ensure Alexander had the advantages of being exposed to the kind of education and culture Philip himself lacked. Aristotle cautioned Alexander that before he was fit to rule he had to experience what it felt like to be ruled. It was a lesson the young prince took to heart.

Alexander developed a love of the arts and, in particular, a great appreciation for the poetry of Homer. He carried a copy of the Homeric epics with him and longed to emulate the feats and lifestyle of his heroes Achilles and Heracles. (Eventually, he would claim descent from both of those Greek heroes- Heracles on his father's side, Achilles, on his mothers).

Philip also made sure Alexander became uncommonly proficient in the use of arms. Indeed he proved to be particularly adept in military matters. At the Battle of Chaeronea, at the age of eighteen, Alexander had led the decisive charge by the Companions cavalry that turned the tide of battle in Philip's favor. Alexander was also, like his father courageous, manipulative and charismatic. Both led their troops from the front and had the wounds to prove it, narrowly escaping death on more than one occasion. Each was able to command immense personal loyalty from the army. Both were able to clothe themselves in the raiment of liberators and became very good in converting those they had defeated into allies and supporters. But Alexander had also inherited and learned traits from his mother and some blamed her for his impetuous streak and, on occasion, his explosive and impulsive temperament.

When Alexander assumed the reins of power he moved quickly to consolidate his position. Almost immediately he had an opportunity to do so. Thebes decided to revolt against his leadership of the League of Corinth and sought supporting allies. Before that support could be mustered Alexander had stormed the city, killed 6000 Thebans and thoroughly sacked the city, sparing only the temples and the house of the poet Pindar and his descendants. He then asked the surrounding neighbors of the Thebans what would be an appropriate punishment for the residents still remaining. With their concurrence, 30,000 survivors were rounded up and sent into slavery. The effect of the incident was to immediately quell any rumblings of revolt, a parallel perhaps to the later concept of killing one admiral to encourage the rest (pour encourager les autres). In a similarly ruthless manner, Cleopatra and her infant daughter, her male relatives and a potential rival for the throne of Macedon were eliminated.

Six months after taking Philip's place, Alexander also took up his cause and led his troops toward the Persian Empire. With his flair for the dramatic, he dragged the reluctant priestess of Delphi into the temple and sought from her a prophecy on his prowess. With her words, "My son, thou art invincible" he headed towards Asia. He followed the reverse of the route that Xerxes had taken in 480 B.C. and at the legendary site of Troy, he offered a sacrifice and donned the bronze armor of Achilles that had been dedicated at the site. The first battle with the

Persians was at the River Granicus and it was there that he inflicted a devastating defeat on the Persians. They had been supported by a contingent of Greek mercenaries who surrendered but to no avail. They were either massacred or sent back to Macedon as slaves, a reminder that Alexander wanted nothing to stand in his way in his march across Asia.

Persian control of the Greek colonies in Asia Minor was totally lost. It didn't take much persuasion for the cities, many of whom had been founded by Greek colonists, to switch their allegiance to Alexander. Remembering the lessons of Aristotle, he treated his new subjects kindly spreading the word that he came not as a conqueror but as a liberator. He did not raise the rate of tribute or taxation as was expected. In Persian cities, he appointed Persian satraps (provincial governors) with the admonition that they had the option between absolute loyalty or death. At Gordium, the ancient capital of Phrygia, inside a temple stood a cart tied to a pole with an intricate, convoluted knot. Legend had it that whoever could untie the knot would rule Asia. Alexander severed it with his sword and headed, confidently, deeper into Asia. As he entered the mountain passes leading into Syria, the Persian Great King Darius moved a huge army up behind Alexander, confident that he had trapped the Macedonian. Alexander was delighted for he realized that the narrow terrain wouldn't allow the Persians to field all of their troops. It was a hard-fought battle, the Battle of Issus, momentum-shifting from side to side, but in the end, Alexander won decisively. Darius fled the battlefield leaving behind in Damascus his mother, his wife, their daughter, ladies-in-waiting and a fortune in gold. Alexander, nursing a thigh wound, retired to Darius' opulent, abandoned tent to celebrate and allow his wound to heal.

Instead of marching eastward into the heart of Persia, Alexander decided to consolidate the territory he had gained. The old city of Tyre fell after a prolonged and brutal siege. Thousands were killed and Roman sources suggest that hundreds were crucified. After that, the residents of Sidon welcomed him with open arms. Then Alexander marched into Egypt where he was given the welcome he expected. Proclaiming him as pharaoh and treating him as divine, the Egyptians avoided any hostilities. Alexander founded a city on the Egyptian coast that he called Alexandria. It was destined to become one of the greatest cities of the Mediterranean. It hosted universities, libraries, the first museum, gymnasia- the best that Greece had to offer the world in terms of arts and culture.

Darius, afraid now of Alexander, sued for peace, offering to share his kingdom with the Macedonian. Alexander would have none of it and at the plain of Gaugamela, in Assyria, the two armies met once more. Again, Alexander was heavily outnumbered (sources suggest it was 5-1 in favor of Darius) but the result was the same as at Granicus and Issus- a decisive victory for Alexander and his army. Darius fled, pursued by the Macedonians. Then one of Darius' cavalry commanders, Bessus, the satrap of Bactria assassinated the Great King and declared himself the new ruler of Persia. Eventually, Alexander caught up to him, cut off his nose and ears and turned him over to his enemies to finish the job. By portraying himself as the avenger of Darius' betrayal, Alexander gained the support of many Persians. He began to wear Persian style clothing and encouraged his soldiers to take Persian women as wives. He himself married Roxane, the daughter of a Bacterian noble. (Later he would marry two Persian princesses, one a daughter of Darius)

After this major battle, Alexander and his army rested and reveled in Babylon, Susa, and Persepolis collecting booty on a grand scale (many millions, if not billions of dollars in today's currency). At Persepolis, following a dare from an Athenian courtesan, Alexander burnt the great palace of Xerxes which he claimed was in revenge for the razing of Athens 150 year's earlier. But plunder was not enough to quench Alexander's thirst for glory. He wanted now to move into India.

A pretext to do so soon presented itself. Two Indian kings were waging war against each other and Alexander allied himself with Taxiles against Porus. It was Alexander's first experience in fighting against elephants but in the Battle of Hydaspes, his army won a crushing victory. Porus was wounded but Alexander was so impressed by his bravery that he gave the king his land back and more besides. Afterward, he pressed on, trying to find the Eastern Ocean, believed, at that time, to be the limit of the world. Then the monsoons hit and after 70 days of relentless rain, his men had had enough. They refused to go on. Alexander sulked in his tent for a couple of days and then accepted the inevitable. They turned back.

Some of the Macedonians, weary of wandering and the rigors of military life, began to plot against Alexander. Alexander's response was quick and, some say, too far-reaching. Long-time supporters were assassinated on the basis of little evidence. Alexander drank excessively and during an argument, in a drunken rage, ran a spear through a cavalry commander who had once saved his life. When a close companion (Hephaistion) of his died of a fever, Alexander's grief knew no bounds. He ordered that a huge monument be erected in his honor and approached the Oracle at Siwa to see if a religious cult could be established in his memory. That request was granted and Alexander celebrated by drinking a huge bowl of undiluted wine. Some say that he died almost immediately; others, that he lingered, speechless, for several days before succumbing to fever (maybe malaria) and, possibly, alcohol poisoning. In any event, tradition says that when he was asked on his deathbed to whom he bequeathed his kingdom, he replied "To the strongest" and expired. He was 33.

The conquests of Alexander created a huge empire and his impact on the world stage is still being debated by historians. Politically his empire would not last beyond the time that it took to create it; culturally this creation became the basis of the Hellenistic age. Historians critical of Alexander portray him as short-sighted and interested only in covering himself with glory for his military exploits while lamenting that there were no more worlds to conquer. The Roman Emperor Augustus felt that Alexander should have found greater satisfaction governing his empire than conquering it. Admirers say that he laid the groundwork for shaping a new political order; it was now up to others to finish the job.

PART 3
CHAPTER 8

Alexander the Great interesting facts and distinctive success values

Alexander the Great born in the city of Pella in central Macedonia in 356 BC, Alexander was the son of King Phillip II and his fourth wife Olympias. He is often referred to as "the Great"for his extraordinary military, strategic and leadership skills. After the death of his father, Alexander crushed internal opposition to ensure complete control over Greece, before he began his renowned campaign which resulted in the conquest of the Achaemenid Empire, one of the most powerful empires in history. At the time of his death, the empire of Alexander covered 5.2 million square kilometers and was the largest state at that time. Furthermore, his conquests led to many repercussions including increased contact and trade between the east and the west.

Alexander the Great interesting facts

Battle of Chaeronea and Defeat of Sacred Band (338 Bc)

The rise of Alexander's father, Philip II of Macedonia, was perceived as a threat by some independent city-states in Greece; principally Thebes and Athens. This led to the Battle of Chaeronea in 338 BC in Boeotia, central Greece; where Alexander at the young age of 18 played a pivotal role, leading the left-wing command to help secure victory for his father. The cavalry wing led by Alexander annihilated the Sacred Band of Thebes, an elite corps previously regarded as invincible. This victory placed Macedonia in a commanding position in Greece enabling the future adventures of Alexander.

Conquest of the Achaemenid Empire –Battle of Gaugamela (331 Bc)

By 331 BC Alexander had crossed the Euphrates and Tigris and moved towards the heart of the Achaemenid Empire. Darius III had by now gathered a huge army including the finest cavalry from his eastern satraps. The armies were face to face in the Battle of Gaugamela in present-day Kurdistan. The Greek army was divided into two parts: the right was commanded by Alexander and the left by his personal friend Parmenion. Darius was in the center with the best of his infantry. The Greek phalanx attacked the center of the enemy lines. Forming a wedge, Alexander struck the weakened center of the Persian army, gaining a clear path to Darius. As the Persian line collapsed, Darius was to flee once again. The Battle of Gaugamela was one of the finest victories of Alexander. Darius was assassinated by one of his own; Bessus. Alexander gained substantial wealth in the Persian capitals of Babylon and Susa; and announced himself the Persian King of Kings.

Reaffirmation of Macedonian Rule as King (336-335 Bc)

After the assassination of Phillip II in 336 BC, Alexander was proclaimed King of Macedonia at the age of 20. The death of Phillip had emboldened many states and tribes; like the Athens, Thessaly, and Thebes; to revolt. Alexander was quick to respond riding with 3000 cavalries south to Thessaly forcing them into surrender. Athens soon came into the fold sending their envoy and, in the city of Corinth, Alexander was given the title 'Hegemon' of the Greek forces against the Persians.

A Winning Strategy is Both Efficient and Innovative

Amazingly, Alexander built his empire with an army that numbered no more than 40,000 men. This means he had to employ his forces to overcome the overwhelming numbers that opposed him. Toward that end, he used terrain, tactics, mobility, and weaponry—including the formidable Macedonian phalanx—to overwhelm his opponents.

In addition, since he could ill afford to detach men from his army to secure his rear lines of communication, he was extraordinarily sympathetic to the people he conquered, going so far as to adopt their dress and customs and even build memorials to their war dead.

Because of this, he was able to recruit indigenous professionals into his governmental structure and leverage their skill and expertise. In effect, he extended the reach of his authority and preserved the core engine of his conquests—his Greek army.

Series of Wins to Ensure Complete Control over Greece (335 Bc)

Before his Asian campaign, Alexander wanted to secure his northern frontiers. He marched north and crushed the Thracian revolts led by Cleitus, King of Illyria, and Glaukias, King of Taulantii among others. These wins were followed by the razing of the city of Thebes, who had revolted again. These victories finally brought the whole of Greece to accept the rule of Alexander. Within just two years Alexander hence ensured complete control over Greece to concentrate his efforts on Asia.

Conquest of the Achaemenid Empire – Battle of the Persian Gate (330 Bc)

In 330 BC, Persian satrap Ariobarzanes led a last stand of the Persian forces in the Battle of Persian Gate in present-day Iran. Alexander was ambushed at a narrow mountain pass (Persian Gate) while traversing to Persepolis; the ceremonial capital of the Persian Empire. Heavy losses were inflicted on the Greek army but after holding the gate for a month, the Persians were finally encircled and defeated. This battle was the last nail in the coffin and Alexander had finally conquered the powerful Achaemenid Empire.

Conquest of the Achaemenid Empire – Battle of the Granicus River (334 Bc)

The Achaemenid Empire (The First Persian Empire) founded by Cyrus the Great was one of the largest empires in history extending from the Balkans and Eastern Europe to Indus in the east. It was managed efficiently through centralized bureaucratic administration using Satraps (similar to the governor of provinces) under the King. As Alexander crossed to Asia a gathering of various Satraps and their forces awaited him at the town of Zelea. The Battle was fought on the banks of the river Granicus near Troy in modern-day Turkey. By fighting on the bank Alexander had minimized the advantage the Persians had in numbers and had rendered their deadly chariots ineffective on soft and muddy soil. Alexander would continue to use this advantage against the Persians and fight many more battles near river banks. Alexander attacked the left with briskness and, making a hole in the center with his wedge formation, he placed his infantry to strike at the Persian army. Several high-ranking Persian nobles were killed by Alexander himself or his horse companions. The battle was over soon.

Seek out the Best Mentors...Then Learn from Them

Alexander had the benefit of being educated in political, military, and cultural matters by excellent tutors including none other than Aristotle.

He also accompanied his father on several military campaigns and distinguished himself in battle at a young age.

He no doubt drew upon that upbringing when he assumed the throne at only 20 years old after Philip was assassinated.

Alexander wasted no time in using his position as general of all Greece to take the strong army his father had left him and expand Greek hegemony into Persia.

Battle of The Hydaspes In Western India (326 Bc)

Alexander had seen the last of the Persian resistance in 328 BC. After his marriage to Roshanak (Roxana) which had cemented his relations with the satrapies of Central Asia, he turned his eyes towards India. Defeating various clans and tribes in the region Alexander crossed the Indus to fight the Battle of Hydrapes against Porus, the ruler of Punjab. An epic battle ensued and Alexander was so impressed by the bravery of Porus that he made an alliance with him, appointing him as the satrap of his own kingdom. This battle was the last among the great battles of Alexander. Besides being a great military tactician and general, Alexander was known for being ruthless, persevering, diplomatic and even kind at some junctures. It was perhaps these qualities that sustained his long and treacherous campaign where he was undefeated in battle.

Conquest of The Achaemenid Empire – Battle of Issus (333 Bc)

After the defeat of the Persians at the Battle of Granicus, Darius III, King of the Achaemenid Empire, cut the Greek line of supply. He then personally gathered a large army setting up a battle with Alexander's army south of the village of Isus. By fighting near river Pinarus, Darius had apparently not analyzed his previous defeat. Alexander was on the unfavorable ground and he instructed his infantry to hold a defensive position. This surprised Darius, who elected to change position and attack the infantry of the Greeks. Alexander and his Royal Companions attacked the left side of the Persian army up the hill. Cutting up the enemy on a restrictive terrain generated a quick retreat. Then Alexander and his elite cavalry led a direct attack on Darius, who was forced to flee. The Battle of Issus is considered as a major breakthrough in Alexander's long campaign against Persia.

The Perils of Professional Excess and Personal Dissipation

As time went on, Alexander's ambition began to grow into megalomania, megalomania fueled by heavy drinking. As his mood became progressively more violent and unstable, those around him came to fear the repercussions of his anger.

As he advanced farther East, Alexander's mental stability progressively eroded. Despite the grave misgivings of his close advisors, he asserted himself as a god. He also held elaborate drinking parties called "symposiums" where wine flowed freely and court sycophants told him how great he was. Alexander drank to stupefying excess.

His ambition, combined with growing paranoia, drove him in search of more glory. In the process of conquering, his drunken excess caused him to burn a city to the ground, execute people who once had been his friends, and force his army on a deadly march through the Iranian desert.

In the end, Alexander became a drunken, mercurial mess. To paraphrase the Good Book, not even the gain of the entire world was able to save his soul.

Alexander the Great Is Regarded As One of the Most Influential People in History

At the time of his death, the empire of Alexander was the largest state of its time covering around 5,200,000 square kilometers (2,000,000 sq mi). His conquests introduced Macedonian rule to several parts of Asia and many of these areas remained under Greek influence for the next two-three centuries. His campaigns also greatly increased contact and trade between east and west. Alexander founded around twenty cities that bore his name. Most prominent among these was Alexandria in Egypt, which became the intellectual and cultural center of the ancient west. Alexander and his exploits were greatly admired in the ancient world, especially by the Roman leaders, who saw him as a role model. Alexander the Great is ranked among the most influential people in history. He has figured in both high and popular culture from his time to this day. Considered among the greatest generals in history, his military tactics are still taught in military academies.

Seige of Tyre and Gaza (332 – 331 Bc)
Alexander had realized that before venturing forth against his enemies he needed to secure his chain of supply. The coastal territories of Palestine, Egypt and Phoenicia were the keys. Tyre, the largest city-state of Phoenicia, refused Alexander's peace proposals claiming that they were neutral in the war. Alexander was, however, unwilling to relent and, in January of 332 BC, he started his long siege of Tyre that lasted almost eight-month. During this time an uncompromising Alexander built bridges to the island city; employed siege machines and fought off the Tyrian navy and army; until the fall of the fort.

After the fall of Tyre, Alexander marched south through Jerusalem to set the siege of Gaza which was a fortified hill. The commander of Gaza, Batis, had refused to surrender to Alexander. After three unsuccessful attempts, Gaza was finally conquered. The fall of Gaza pushed Alexander into Egypt where he was seen more as a liberator. Here, in 331 BC, he founded the city of Alexandria, which would become the center of Hellenistic culture and commerce in times to come.

Alexander the Great distinctive success values

Alexander the Great, one of the most successful and inspirational leaders in history, ruled the Empire of Macedon. His empire stretched from Europe to India and created a legacy that many looked to emulate and, more importantly, attempted to claim.

Today, Macedonia's geography is disputed and, much like the Balkan's, its location depends on whom you ask.

Two regions identify as "Macedonia" – one is a province in northern Greece and the other is an actual country, with its official name being the Republic of Macedonia. When Yugoslavia split and each region became its own separate state – the Republic of Macedonia is one of them – Greece did not recognize the newly formed state by its constitutional name. Instead, they use the term FYROM, short for Former Yugoslav Republic of Macedonia, as they want to clearly distinguish between the two.

People who identify as Macedonian in both regions share a language, culture, and unique traditions that set them apart from neighboring nations. Many view the border between Greece and the Republic of Macedonia as an unnatural partition between the Macedonian people. The border that is separating a group of people that long to hold onto their traditions has created a name dispute that acts as a political lock on Greek and Macedonian advancement.

Greece views the term "Macedonians" as all Greek citizens living in the province of Macedonia while seeing their northern neighbor's name as a threat to Greek territory, history, and culture. It views citizens of the Republic of Macedonia as Slavs instead of sharing a bloodline with Macedonians, and feel that as long as the nation uses the name Macedonia and celebrates Macedonian history, it is stealing a part of Greek culture. Naturally, Macedonians perceive their identity as being restricted and pushed aside. They interpret that their history of thousands of years is restricted to the 40-plus years as a member of Yugoslavia. Ongoing disputes have politically handicapped Macedonia, as Greece boycotted the Republic of Macedonia's entrance into the EU and NATO. Greece also made the United Nations recognize its northern neighbors as FYROM, much to the dismay of the Republic of Macedonia.

Identity Formation

The identity of the Balkans remains confused and at time's inconsistent. On one hand, all the nations share similar cultural aspects, and yet Serbo-Croatian, Albanian, Greek, and Romanian are all completely unrelated languages. They all share a common history of war and occupation with varying degrees of successful empire-building, and yet they share different religions, different allies, different objectives, and consistently shifting borders. How do Balkan nations find a new identity that allows them to communicate and connect with Western Europe? When the world thinks of anything east of Germany, they imagine the remnants of the USSR. In reality, seven nations in the Balkans thought to have been under the Soviet regime never were, and they would prefer to be likened to Greece – a nation in the Balkans known to never be under the USSR. In this sense, the general identity that they share is viewed incorrectly.

Some Balkan nations are hesitant to acknowledge that Western civilization has made drastic improvements to their way of life for fear of losing their own culture. In the Balkans, there is difficulty distinguishing between globalization and Westernization, and this precisely makes it difficult to form a much-needed new identity. Outside the Balkans, there is a distinct separation of ability between the West discovering problems in the region and the West solving problems in the region.

In this case, the West is right to condemn ethnic nationalism considering that it delays Balkan progression. However, nationalism has created an illusion about Balkan citizens and led to the West asserting to changing the Balkans according to an external vision rather than build a system based on existing identity structures. On moral grounds, ethnic nationalism should be condemned, but it is important to understand the dynamics of Macedonian identity are so complex that ethnicity either affirms or denies social rights, depending arbitrarily on the circumstances of location.

If the West doesn't understand the citizens in Greece and Macedonia, as most claim it does not, then an ethical question needs to be raised regarding any EU and NATO requirements imposed on the Republic of Macedonia that is influenced by Greece. In this atmosphere, the current verbal civil war will continue with newly cemented nationalistic markers on both sides; statues, monuments, and museums will continue to be built for future Greek and Macedonian citizens perpetuating its stories.

Macedonia, in a democratic fashion, has asked for inclusion into the new world and is ready to develop through a fair checklist of responsibilities. Forming a new identity while curbing nationalism is important for the Balkans, but there is no way for the EU to morally contains one nationality, Macedonian, for the preference of the other, Greek. For the West to allow Greece to restrict Macedonia's development is contradictory to the values they represent; this is what Macedonians are waiting for the West to realize.

Communicating with the West

Due to the importance of the region in terms of incoming refugees, Greece and Macedonia have had to work together more than ever. To support their story during a sensitive period, the Greek Ministry of Foreign Affairs recently published a report on the issue here. However, Greek ministers have succumbed to Freudian slips and even referred to FYROM as the Republic of Macedonia, causing public outrage in Greece.

Naturally, the West sees something inherently fascinating about a nation holding back the development of another over a name dispute. But because Greece is a part of the Western world, it does not allow Macedonia to enter into important Western institutions. Both are now brothers in crime, perpetually in a lose-lose situation that has the world asking, "What's in a name?"

For Macedonia to ever develop and become something respected by the Western world, it needs to adhere to guidelines and policies influenced by its Greek neighbors. Since Macedonia is not permitted to enter NATO or the EU, even though its population overwhelmingly supports accession, and the political consciousness of that state is interpreted as being trivial compared to Western nations. To ever make gradual steps toward globalization, Macedonia is required to do the unthinkable: effectively reconfigure its identity and revise what makes it uniquely Macedonian.

When the hurdles are insuperable and come far too early, it ruins political innovation. The West must not think of Macedonia as a nation too stubborn to change its name even though it holds back development. Rather, they must ask: what motivation do Macedonian politicians have for making improvements if you consistently ask them to lose their identity?

Alexander the Great is a case in point. He conquered most of the known world before most people today are out of college and into their first job. In an amazing eleven-year journey of conquest—unparalleled in the history of the world—he rode more than 10,000 miles, fought 70 battles without losing a single one and conquered from Egypt to India.

Alexander accomplished greater deeds than, not only of the kings who had lived before him but also of those who were to come later down to our time. Alexander the Great was born at Pella Macedonia in 356 B.C.E. He spent his childhood years watching his father transforming Macedonia into a great military power. His father was King Phillip and his mother was Olympias. His mother was the princess of neighboring Epirus. She was a deeply spiritual who taught her son about his ancestors such as Achilles and Hercules. From his earliest ages, then he was conditioned for conquest and glory in being a king. He then became focused on becoming a great ruler, which he soon will become.

As a young boy, Alexander was fearless and strong. At the age of 12, he tamed a beautiful horse by the name of Bucephalus, a horse than no one else could ride. His father was so proud of him and his horsemanship. Aristotle came to Pella in 343 at Phillips bidding to direct education towards his son. Alexander was taught by him from the age of thirteen to sixteen. Alexander was taught by Aristotle at the Mieza Temple. Alexander was told to have had a strong athletic build but was shorter than the average Macedonian. He had fair skin and was clean-shaven most of the time. He had green eyes and was said to be a very handsome man. When leading his army he would always wear something very recognizable from long distances by his enemies? Alexander wore two large white plumes in his hat to distinguish himself from the other soldiers during battle. While not in battle, the Macedonian usually wore Persian clothing, at least during his late twenties and early thirties. His silk Persian clothing had a long robe, cape, sash and headband in the royal purple and white colors.

Alexander the Great respected women and treated them fairly. Aristotle's early teachings may have had something to do with Alexander's thoughts toward women. When taking a young woman captive after overtaking a city, he would protect them from his troops, and treat them as if they were his daughters. Often, when talking to older queens, Alexander would refer to them as a mother, showing his respect to them as if being a part of his close family. One of Alexander's finest acts was when he took his enemy Darius' mother and other family members when he conquered Persia: thinking that Alexander was going to kill them; Darius was much relieved to find that Alexander treated them royally and with respect as guests of his kingdom.

Alexander the Great Alexander was a great Greek king. As a military commander, he was undefeated and the most successful throughout history. On his way home from conquering many countries, he came down with an illness. At that moment, his captured territories, powerful army, sharp swords, and wealth all had no meaning to him. He realized that death would soon arrive and he would be unable to return to his homeland. He told his officers: "I will soon leave this world. I have three final wishes. You need to carry out what I tell you." His generals, in tears, agreed.

"My first wish is to have my physician bring my coffin home alone. After a gasping for air, Alexander continued: "My second wish has scattered the gold, silver, and gems from my treasure-house along the path to the tomb when you ship my coffin to the grave." After wrapping in a woolen blanket and resting for a while, he said: "My final wish it to put my hands outside the coffin." People surrounding him all were very curious, but no one dares to ask the reason. Alexander's most favored general kissed his hand and asked: "My Majesty, We will follow your instruction. But can you tell us why you want us to do it this way?" After taking a deep breath, Alexander said: "I want everyone to understand the three lessons I have learned. To let my physician carry my coffin alone is to let people realize that a physician cannot really cure people's illness. Especially when they face death, the physicians are powerless. I hope people will learn to treasure their lives. My second wish is to tell people not to be like me in pursuing wealth. I spent my whole life pursuing wealth, but I was wasting my time most of the time. My third wish to let people understand that I came to this world in empty hands and I will leave this world also in empty hands." he closed his eyes after finished talking and stopped breathing.

CHAPTER 9

Alexander the Great Final Days

However, death prevented him to launch a new expedition. Alexander the Great died in June 323 BC in his palace in Babylon from unknown causes. It could be poisoning, or malaria or even a physical problem that may have caused the death of Alexander. Others say that he died from grief because his companion, Hephaestion, had been killed in a battle a few months ago.

When he died, his wife Roxana was pregnant to their son but Alexander didn't see his heir being born. After his death, the vast Empire he has created, the Empire that was stretching from Greece and Egypt to India, was split into four parts and was divided to his generals, while his son was killed before adulthood.

Despite his just 33 years of life, Alexander had seen them all in life: love and hate, loyalty and conspiracy, war and peace, virtues and faults. He was happy to fulfill his ambitions and he changed history and the fate of many tribes, as the Greek civilization was spread far and wide. The cities he had conquered and established flourished for many centuries and even today there are tribes in Asia that say they descend from Alexander the Great.

After his death, nearly all the noble Susa marriages dissolved, which shows that the Macedonians despised the idea. There never came to unity between Macedonians and Persians and there wasn't even unity among the Macedonians. Alexander's death opened the anarchic age of the Successors and a bloody Macedonian civil war for power followed. As soon as the news of Alexander's death was known, the Greeks rebelled yet again and so begun the Lamian War. The Macedonians were defeated and expelled from Greece, but then Antipater received reinforcements from Craterus who brought to Macedonia the 10,000 veterans discharged at Opis. Antipater and Craterus jointly marched into Greece, defeated the Greek army at Cannon in Thessaly and brought the war to an end. Greece will remain under Macedonian rule for the next one and a half-century. In Asia, the Macedonian commanders who served Alexander fought each other for power. Perdiccas and Meleager were murdered, Antigonus rose to control most of Asia, but his growth of power brought the other Macedonian generals in the coalition against him. He was killed in battle and the Macedonian Empire split into four main kingdoms - the one of Seleucus (Asia), Ptolemy (Egypt), Lysimachus (Thrace), and Antipater's son Cassander (Macedonia, including Greece). The rise of Rome put an end to Macedonian kingdoms. Macedonia and Greece were conquered in 167/145 BC, Seleucid Asia by 65 BC, and Cleopatra VII, the last Macedonian descendent of Ptolemy committed suicide in 30 BC, after which Egypt was added to the Roman Empire.

With the split of the Roman Empire into Western and Eastern (Byzantium), the Macedonians came to play a major role in Byzantium. The period of rule of the Macedonian dynasty which ruled the Eastern Roman Empire from 867 to 1056 is known as the "Golden Age" of the Empire. The Eastern Roman Empire fell in the 15th century and Macedonia, Greece, and the whole southern Balkans came under the rule of the Turkish Empire.

CHAPTER 10

CONCLUSION

Alexander the Great subjugated the Persian Empire and large portions of western India in only eleven years. Scholars have speculated on aspects of Alexanderís campaign, some attributing his success to tyche or fortune, others to Alexanderís debt to his father, Philip II of Macedon and still others assert that Alexander held a philosophical belief that he was duty-bound to save the barbarians from themselves. He was not at every point of his journey infallible. Alexander the Great committed atrocities, he enslaved large groups of his enemies and he may have been responsible for the deaths of many of his own troops. However, these events are just sidelights to what would become his greatest accomplishment, the consolidation, and administration of the largest empire that had yet been seen. The major argument throughout this study shows that after 330 BC, with the fall of the last of the Achaemenids, Alexander focused on acculturation and absorption of the Persian Empire; he was not (as scholars have argued) a servant of tyche or devoid of thought concerning a large, sustained empire.

It is quite clear that Alexander diverged from the common Greco-Macedonian tradition of prejudice and xenophobia. His actions and their consequences remain a testament to his foresight and flexibility. The sources document loud opposition to Alexanderís innovative policies, illustrating the concerns felt by his compatriots. Alexander heard consternation and asked for his troopsí trust in those matters. Some modern scholars have argued that Alexander could not abandon these provocative policies because he was consumed with self-interest. It seems that their conclusions are based upon a comparison with the former kings of Macedon. Because Alexander did not follow a traditional Greco-Macedonian style of rule it is thought that he must have been unjustified in his actions. That Alexander was different from his predecessors is undeniable, but this does not in itself mean that he was abandoning his heritage. Although he would not be bound too tightly by the traditions of his fathers before him, Alexander throughout the entire campaign strove to maintain strong ties with his companions.

Alexander used three key component policies to form the conquered territory into what he thought would be the most secure realm. He appointed Persian satrap's to administer Persian populations. He cemented his bond with the most influential Persians and the lowliest peasants with imagery they could recognize. Finally, he had his most important Companions married to the daughters of noteworthy Persian aristocrats. The sources agree on the substance of each of these decisions, if not on the motivation for them. No treatment of the main period of greek civilization should end without emphasizing the continuity both with what went before and with what came after. Continuity is clearest in the sphere of religion, which may be said to have been "embedded" in Greek life. Some of the gods alleged to have been relatively late imports into Greece can, in fact, be shown to have Mycenaean origins. For instance, one Athenian myth held that Dionysus was a latecomer, having been introduced into Attica from Eleuthera in the 6th century. There is a reference to Dionysus (or di-wo-no-so-jo), however, on Linear B tablets from the 2nd millennium BCE. Looking forward, Dionysus's statue was to be depicted in a grand procession staged in Alexandria in the 3rd century BCE by Ptolemy II Philadelphus. (The iconographic significance of the king's espousal of Dionysus becomes clear in light of the good evidence that in some sense Alexander the Great had identified himself with Dionysus in Carmania.) Nor was classical Dionysus confined to royal exploitation: it has been shown that the festivals of the City Dionysia at Athens and the deme festival of the Rural Dionysia were closely woven into the life of the Athenian empire and the Athenian state. Another Athenian, Euripides, represented Dionysus in a less tame and "official" aspect in the Bacchae; the Euripidean Dionysus has more in common with the liberating Dionysus of Carmania or with the socially disruptive Dionysus whose worship the Romans in 186 BCE were to regulate in a famous edict. The longevity and multifaceted character of Dionysus symbolizes the tenacity of the Greek civilization, which Alexander had taken to the banks of the Oxus but which in many respects still carried the marks of its Archaic and even prehistoric origins.

Made in the USA
Monee, IL
04 August 2020